CONFESSIONS OF AN ESPORTS MOM

Transforming a Parent's Perspective About Video Gaming

Karen Quinones-Smith

CONFESSIONS OF AN ESPORTS MOM:
Transforming a Parent's Perspective on Video Gaming
www.confessionsofanesportsmom.online

Paperback ISBN: 979-8-862029-52-9

References to internet websites (URLs) were accurate at the time of writing. Authors and the publishers are not responsible for URLs that may have expired or changed since the manuscript was prepared.

Limits of Liability and Disclaimer of Warranty
The author and publisher shall not be liable for your misuse of the enclosed material. This book is strictly for informational and educational purposes only.

Warning – Disclaimer
The purpose of this book is to educate and entertain. The author and/or publisher do not guarantee that anyone following these techniques, suggestions, tips, ideas, or strategies will become successful. The author and/or publisher shall have neither liability nor responsibility to anyone with respect to any loss or damage caused, or alleged to be caused, directly or indirectly by the information contained in this book.

Publisher
10-10-10 Publishing, Markham, ON Canada

Printed in Canada and the United States of America

Dedication

To my sons, this book is dedicated to you. Because of you and your passion for the world of Esports, I transformed into the person I am today. Thank you for showing me and inspiring me to learn something new.

To my husband, thank you for lifting me up when I stumbled and couldn't find my way. You encouraged me to find new innovative ways to bring Esports to the community.

To my friends, you have been my unwavering support system. When I knew nothing about the world of Esports, you stood by me. I know I drove you crazy, but somehow, I have managed to get you hooked and now you are watching Esports.

A big thank you to all the parents who don't quite understand Esports but are willing to learn and support their children. Your efforts to connect to your child and bridge that generational gap mean more than you know.

To all the gamers patiently teaching their parents about the world of Esports, you are doing an incredible job! Your dedication is truly inspiring, and you are making a difference.

Lastly, I want to thank the Esports community. I am grateful for every single one of you. We have had fantastic late-night conversation, early morning coffee, monthly check-ins, behind the scenes interviews, creative lunches, and incredible collaborations. I appreciate you for showing me the way and helping me rise like a phoenix. Let's continue to Bridge the Gap together.

Table of Contents

Foreword

Do you have a gamer? Are you having difficulties getting them off video games? Do you understand the esports world and the benefits? Would you like to be able to talk to your child about Esports?

Confessions of an Esports Mom was written to let you know that you are not alone in the gaming world. Karen Quinones-Smith is a mom of gamers, and her journey takes you through her winding unraveling process in the world of Esports. She was unknowingly being molded into the person she is today.

Karen's unwillingness to accept Esports into her life made her stronger for the time when she had the epiphany that the world of Esports is where she belongs. After she had a clear understanding of Esports, she built a business called Bridging the Gap in Esports, and now she goes out into the community and across the United States to talk about it.

Her passion continues to grow as the world of Esports evolves. Everything she does is innovative and engaging. Read this mom's journey through the magical world of Esports. Then, after you read it, contact her. She is always ready to talk about Esports, and she might tell you things that were not mentioned in the book.

I can't wait to see what she does next.

Raymond Aaron
***New York Times* Bestselling Author**

Chapter 1

Preparing for the Cruise

Finding a Cruise to Take

In the spring of 2005, I started to look at different cruise lines to go on a family vacation in the winter, and I wanted to make it perfect. I have been on many cruises before, and they were always in winter. It is a magical time of the year and this time it was going to be spectacular because I would be with my family. I searched for a cruise line that would cater to my children. I was amazed at how many activities they had for them. We never had to leave the ship. But there was one cruise line that stuck out more than the others. So, this Disney girl started to dive deep into the Disney Cruise Line.

I started to research every detail. I looked at all excursions, and Wow! They even had a private island. I was feeling so good about this trip, so I added a few days at the Animal Kingdom resort. This was going to be phenomenal. Every detail was calculated, and I was getting excited about the trip. I told my husband that I was going to confirm the trip and he said to wait a minute. "Wait for what?" I asked. I had no idea what he was going to say. He said, "I told some of my coworkers about the cruise and they want to go on a cruise with us." I said, "Fine, here are the details; they can join us. It will be fun."

My husband looked at me puzzled and said, "No, they want to go on a cruise in August." I sighed and took a deep breath. They did not want to go on a cruise with us; they just wanted to go on a cruise. He knows I don't like to go on a cruise during hurricane season. I said, "You go, I am not going on a cruise in August. I am not going." He went on to say that this was a great opportunity for him to have fun with his coworkers and get a better post. I knew he was tired of working on his post, but I didn't know he wanted to leave. His facial expressions were unwavering, and he was excited to go on a vacation with his coworkers. I rolled my eyes and said, "Okay, okay, I will look into it." Sometimes you have to pick and choose your battles.

Word of the cruise spread like wildfire at his job. They were having meetings and my input was not taken into consideration. I was the only one that had been on the cruise before, but that didn't matter; and since I did not work in the same place as my husband, I could not voice my opinion. My trip was completely hijacked, and they were quickly making decisions and doing it all wrong.

I told my husband that I did not like this and I was not happy. This was supposed to be our vacation and I did all the work already. Did I make a mistake by saying Okay? This was not what I wanted. I guess I was just going to have to roll with it.

With the burden of having to help plan a cruise out of my hands, I took the opportunity to work on my "Mommy homework program." "Mommy homework" was curriculum I created for my children to give them a head start and a strong educational foundation. As they mastered every challenge I gave them; I pushed them further while making it fun. My children were only toddlers (two and three years old) but they were already reading, writing, doing math, and identifying colors and animals. "Mommy homework" was a game changer. Looking back, I should have sold my program—maybe I still can?

One evening while my children were reading to me, my husband walked in and said he had an announcement: We (his coworkers) took a vote and decided to go on the cruise on August 28, 2005. I laughed; a vote, really! This group never agreed on anything. I knew it was the alpha of the group and his wife making all the decisions. I shook my head and turned my attention back to my children.

A few days later, my husband told me that they wanted to block cabins together, and that's where I drew the line. I was not going to be in a tiny little cabin with two small children and a huge double stroller. I needed a family friendly haven, a place with a lot of space for us to unwind from the day. I stood firm booked a different cabin.

The next thing I heard was they were fighting over the excursions. What was going on? I took my control back and booked our excursions without them. I was back on top. My excitement for the cruise started to grow and it was time to shop! I was channeling my inner Flintstone. CHARGE IT!

Concerns About the Cruise

When planning a trip that takes you away from your familiar surroundings, it is only natural for you to have some concerns about your safety. As a law enforcement officer, safety is always a priority because the unknown can be overwhelming. And if that wasn't enough for you to be concerned about, throw in the unpredictable weather, like a hurricane. And being on the high seas changes everything. How do you prepare for that? How do you control that? Honestly, you only have control over your reaction in any situation.

One of my biggest fears is giving up control, whether it's boarding a plane, stepping onto a cruise ship, hopping on a bus, or even getting into an Uber. You are entrusting your safety to someone else and placing your life in their hands.

Now, you may be wondering why on earth I was willing to subject myself to this, especially when I still had so many concerns swirling in my head. The answer is simple: I love my husband and I love to travel, but I knew I would be on emotional roller coaster. It's just my makeup. Being nervous keeps me on my toes with a clear view of my surroundings.

I did not want to go on a cruise in August. It just makes sense to escape to a tropical paradise when your hometown is under several inches or even feet of snow. This was going to be a challenge for me, but as a wife and a mother, I wanted our family to be happy. I decided to sacrifice my feelings so that my husband could be with his friends. I can hear you in the background telling me to let him go alone. Trust me, I did think about it. I even said it out loud, but I wanted to go on a vacation, and I didn't have enough vacation time to go on two cruises.

If anything were to happen, I have more than enough confidence in our professional training to navigate the family to safety. Nevertheless, the thought of cruising during hurricane season still weighed heavily on my heart. It was like getting in line for a ride while anticipating your turn. With every step you take, the screams seem to get louder, haunting you to get out of the line and go home.

Hurricane Season

As the summer months rolled in quickly, and the arrival of the Atlantic hurricane season began, the air became thick like the haze that consumed us from the Canadian fire on June 6, 2023. I kept listening with anticipation to the weather reports. I was curious about what was going to happen. The weather forecasters were painting a clear picture of how the tropical storms and hurricanes were wreaking havoc throughout the Caribbean and off the coast of Florida. Well, as fate would have it, there was a hurricane arriving in the United States at the time of our cruise. The very thing I was afraid of was coming true. Maybe I was thinking about this too much and put it into existence.

The weeks that led up to the cruise were intense. There had been eight hurricanes, four tropical storms, and even a tropical depression. Every time I heard the announcement of an approaching hurricane or storm, it sent a shiver down my spine. I found myself grinding my teeth and praying for everyone's safety. It was an emotional roller coaster, and I was reminded of how we are not in control.

August 28, 2005, was getting closer, and the hurricane was on its way to the United States. Then it was given a name. It was called Katrina. It was a force of nature that was on a course to hit Louisiana, and it was going to affect the waters in the Gulf. This is why I did not want to go on a cruise in August. It is ludicrous. I became consumed with the weather report and was looking for updates on the storm every minute, hoping it would not touch the United States.

I talked about my concerns with my husband, who dismissed them with a shrug. In his mind, hurricanes were unpredictable and all we could do was wait it out. I had lost total control of the situation, and I did not like it.

Mixed emotions filled the air as we got closer to the departure date and Hurricane Katrina continued her journey towards the United States. Everyone was silent. The airlines didn't say anything, nor did the cruise line. I was frustrated. I couldn't help but wonder that if we had chosen to sail on the fabulous Disney Cruise Line, they would have reached out to us by now, and perhaps we would have received a call from Mickey Mouse himself.

I was sitting in a world of uncertainty, and I could not take it anymore. I called the cruise line to get some clarity. They said they were waiting to see which way Hurricane Katrina was going. They did not have a contingency plan at this time. So, I called the airline and they said all flights going to Florida were on time. Well, those calls didn't help me! I was stuck in the abyss of the unknown. All I wanted to hear was, if this happened, we would have to do this or that. Simple! Feeling lost, I gave my children their "Mommy homework." Watching them do "Mommy homework" made me feel better as it encouraged them to discover more.

Going to the Airport

The day had finally arrived, and the excitement was bubbling inside of me. I don't know if it was because we were going to have a good time or because the impending hurricane was moving quickly towards the United States. We had not heard a word from the cruise line or the airline. The unknown was unsettling.

The sun had not come up yet and I was wishing I could stay in my cozy bed. But instead, I was securing my children in the car and just like that we were on our way to conquer the airport and get through the security line. The trip to the airport seemed longer than usual. What was taking so long? There was no traffic. My children did not notice anything; they were playing on their Leapster.

As we got closer to the airport, my stomach started to do somersaults. I was so nervous, and still, nothing from the airlines or the cruise line. It was like we were playing a game, and I was definitely losing. We arrived at the airport, and I took a deep breath, mentally preparing myself for the airport madness. I put both Leapters in my carry-on bag and walked toward the entrance. My husband was talking to the bag handler, hoping they wouldn't lose our luggage—it has happened before. With determination on our faces, we walked through the entrance and headed towards the dreaded security checkpoint. I was not ready for this.

There was something really eerie about the airport that day. It was so empty. I felt like I was in a horror movie, and I am not a fan of horror movies. I started to look around for the EXIT signs. I would be the first one to get out of there with my family. I thought airports were always busy, but I guess they were not. The security checkpoint was faster than I thought it would be, there was no one on line.

The next thing I knew we were on our way to the gate and just as we sat down, the sun started to rise, and a beautiful rainbow illuminated the sky with its brilliant colors. I can remember it like it was yesterday. There is something about sunrises and rainbows that bring out the goodness in everyone. I wondered if this was a sign. Were we going to be, OK?

The airport started filling up with passengers ready to go off to hundreds of destinations, and my children asked for their Leapters, of course. Leapster was a great invention. It was a handheld educational device. Children can learn math, reading, and writing through fun, interactive play. It captivated children and motivated them to learn without knowing they are learning. I love this device; it was reinforcing everything I was teaching them in “Mommy homework.”

I looked around, trying to spot my husband’s coworkers, who had made all the plans. Where were they? I thought we were on the same flight. But they were nowhere to be found. Seriously? Were they playing hide and seek? Did they forget? Anything’s possible with that group.

After making a few calls, someone finally answered their phone. They had just arrived at the airport. By this time the airport was bustling with people and it was going to take them a long time to get through the security check point. I just shook my head in disbelief. So much for the well-coordinated group trip! I just let it go and focused on the more important things like feeding my hungry children and trying to get them to put down their Leapters for a few minutes.

I Hate to Fly but I Do

As my husband and I watched the rainbow disappear into the sky, we heard an announcement over the loudspeaker: "All passengers with small children, and others who need assistance, can board the plane now." Why don't they say that when you're getting off the plane? We gathered our things and headed towards the gate. The sounds of all the people chattering in the airport started to fade away. I was excited. When we arrived at the plane door, I rubbed the side of the plane gently and said a quick prayer. It sounds strange but it has become a comforting habit that I have done for years, and it has not failed me yet!

My children hopped onto the plane, and you could see the excitement on their faces. We were starting on a journey that would bring us cherished memories, no matter what happens. We rushed to our seats, trying not to hold up any other passengers. Once we were in our seats, I handed both of them their Leapsters. Do you see what was happening? I did not see it. Can you see the pattern that was starting? I didn't.

We were all buckled in, and the plane started its push back from the gate. The engine started to roar, and as we began to move slowly down the runway, my heart began to flutter. I was holding on to my children when the captain's voice echoed through the cabin, and he said that name I did not want to hear, Katrina! What was Katrina doing now? The captain stated that we would be landing on time in Tampa. Katrina had changed direction and we were going to stay on course. This was not comforting at all. Everybody kept telling me, hurricanes are unpredictable. When did that change? I didn't want to think about being a speck in the sky with the impending hurricane headed our way. But I did.

The plane raced down the runway and picked up speed, just like the thoughts in my head. I held on to my children tightly. They didn't have a care in the world; all they needed was their Leapters. I braced myself for the lift off and I let go of my control and gave it to the pilot.

As we lifted up into the sky, there was a hint of gloom that filled the cabin. I think everybody was worried about Hurricane Katrina, but as the sound of the engine got louder and we rose further from the Earth, you could hear people starting to talk and enjoy the flight. Laughter started to fill the cabin. Everyone started to relax and enjoy the flight. Thanks to the great flight attendance that kept us calm.

Landing and the Cruise

Once we landed in Tampa, I could not wait to put my feet on solid ground. I wanted to kiss the ground. But I didn't. We waited for everyone to get off the plane before we left. When we walked to the baggage claim; there was some commotion near the cruise line employee. Apparently, the cruise line had a contingency plan and never told us prior to arriving at the Tampa airport. I could hear everybody whispering as the cruise line employee came closer to us. My husband went to get the bags and I went to hear what the employee had to say, with my children.

By the time I got to the employee, she had already told many of the passengers what was going to happen. That was when another passenger came from behind me and asked the employee, "What is going on?" The cruise line employee explained that there was a change. You could tell she was struggling to tell us because we were going to encounter a long bus ride and many of the passengers would be upset. She stated that our ship was not in Tampa; it was in Fort Lauderdale, because of Katrina. This was an interesting twist. Consistent with cruise line enthusiasm, she stated we would have to take the bus to the ship. The enthusiasm quickly left her voice when she said it would be a four-hour trip. Take a deep breath, Karen; you got this. You have Leapsters and great snacks. It will be fine. I could not help thinking about the look on my husband's coworkers' faces when they found out they had a four-hour trip to the ship. This would not have ever happened in the winter months.

If any of you have been on a trip with toddlers, in a small, confined place for hours, you know this was going to be a challenge. These tiny humans filled with energy were going to monopolize this experience. More than half of the people getting on the bus were still half sleep, but my children's sparkling energy was ready to explode.

It was like musical chairs as we entered the bus; everyone started moving around in hopes that these small humans would not be next to them. Finally, we saw four vacant seats and they were together. I quickly spotted a group of ladies that were sitting right behind the empty seats. They appeared to be on a girl's trip. I could hear them whispering, "This is going to be the longest four hours ever." I don't know what they were expecting from my children. I don't know what kind of chaos they thought my children were going to cause. I did not engage. And for those of you who know me, you know how hard that was. I didn't want to make the four-hour trip seem longer.

It seemed like forever, waiting for passengers to get on the bus. Finally, we departed the airport. My husband's coworkers did not make our bus. We sat back and started to enjoy the ride. For a while, we looked at all the sights that Tampa had to offer, and then they said it: "Can we have our Leapsters?" My children dove into their Leapsters, maneuvering through every question and getting them right. About 30 minutes later, I watched as the Leapsters slowly slipped out of their tiny hands and onto their laps as they fell asleep. I waited a few minutes to remove the Leapsters, and they were asleep for hours.

When the bus pulled into the port at Fort Lauderdale, we waited for everyone to get off the bus, but as the ladies who sat behind us walked past, they thanked us for having well-behaved children. They were marveling over the great behavior our children had displayed, and with a mischievous smile on my face, because I couldn't resist, I said, "You thought this was going to be a horrible ride on the bus. I hope you ladies have a great cruise." Truth be told, I didn't think it was going to be that smooth either. I was so proud of them.

We walked onto the magnificent ship with our camera in hand. Yes, I said camera. Cell phones weren't smart back then. What happened when we first got on the ship is a little blurry; I don't remember if we were even looking for my husband's coworkers, or if we were just having fun exploring the ship. Anyway, we were having a good time before the ship sailed.

We found a spot to watch as the ship pulled out of the port, and the lovely ladies from the bus came over and said hello. We decided to watch the ship sail away together, and we were off on a new adventure. As the ship got further away from the land, and the seas became choppy, I got seasick for a few hours, but then it was smooth sailing. We ran into the ladies from the bus a lot. We ate dinner together almost every night and we went on a lot of excursions together. If I recall correctly, we only saw my husband's coworkers 2 times while on the ship: when they came to the kiddie pool, and at the Midnight Dance contest, which my younger son won!

The cruise was magnificent despite my initial concerns. Leapster was my saving grace on that bus, so when I got home, I went straight to Toys R Us and bought enough cartridges to keep them entertained for years. Who would have thought that this was the beginning of an Esports path.

I don't want to leave out the ladies from the bus. We became good friends on the cruise ship, and we stayed friends for eight or nine years afterwards. They all lived two towns over from me. But life got in the way and we lost contact. I wonder how they're doing and if they're still going on cruises together.

As far as my husband changing his post, I made a call and got him into another command. I didn't want to do it, but I did. Old school law enforcement know that you only use your hook for emergencies. I took my chances and used my hook. I know I could have done that in the beginning and kept my Disney trip. Glad to say, it all worked out and I never went on a cruise during hurricane season again.

Chapter 2

The Grooming Begins

Missing the Game Boy Phase

My knowledge of handheld gaming devices was limited. Leapster was my go-to, and it was all I knew. Because of my children's ages, we missed the whole Game Boy phase. I don't know if that was good or bad, but I do not think it made a difference. Everything I knew was going to change when my older son started school. There was a handheld device called Nintendo DS Lite; this was going to forever revolutionize everything in our household.

I was still trying to hold on to the Leapster, but I quickly learned that I was going to lose this battle. The interest for my children to play the Nintendo DS Lite grew rapidly. The Nintendo DS Lite was not cheap and I had to buy two. I had some concerns about the game. I did not know how to play, but my children learned how to play quickly on their own and became experts.

Parents started to dislike gaming, and most of them didn't like it because they didn't understand it. As for me, I was going with the flow. How bad could it be? It was a little handheld device. They kept playing and I kept purchasing cartridges to feed their gaming frenzy. I still had control because they were still engaged in physical activities such as soccer and karate, and we had a good balance.

But those innocent screens became extremely captivating, and I failed to see any problems. I was optimistic, and I trusted our well-rounded lifestyle. I didn't have to set any limitations or boundaries. I thought this was just going to be a phase and it would just go away like everything else.

As the days went on there was something deep down in my gut telling me that there was more than what I could see but how harmful could it be? It was something they could hold in their hands—how much control could this small game have over my children's lives? I just kept sweeping it under the rug. I was just like ostrich with my head in the sand.

Buying Consoles

Our next adventure took us on an exciting journey with the Wii console. This time, I didn't have to buy two. One for the entire family. I liked the Wii console; it promoted physical activity. Yes, not every game was physical, and you had to sit and play games like Mario Kart, but for the most part, you were on your feet. We played together all the time. It brought us closer and we had a lot of fun. Mama Bear was happy.

From the very beginning, I have to confess that Mario Kart and I had a very rocky relationship. No matter how hard I tried those tricky turns, those banana peels would come out of nowhere and they were annoying. My children wanted to know how I could even drive a car if I couldn't drive in the game. I have to admit, I was wondering the same thing.

One of my favorite parts of the Wii experience was the tournaments we created. Everybody had a game they were good at. So, everyone would have wins and losses. We encouraged each other to do better and have fun. I even videotaped us playing, so that we could play it back and laugh.

New games were released, and our library of Wii games expanded. However, my children grew weary of playing with their parents when the Xbox 360 was released. It was time to move on and they left us for a new gaming adventure.

How was I going to control this? I did not think I had anything to worry about. They were involved in a lot of academic clubs and traditional sports that they loved. They wouldn't have any time to play video games. So, I waited until they asked; and yes, I bought one console. This was going to be different for us, and I would have to figure it out. How was I going to protect them, and what was I going to be protecting them from? I guess the gaming stigma!

We all know that gamers have a negative stigma attached to them. I was getting worried that my children would be looked upon the same way. I remember people telling me that gaming "would melt your brain" or "diminish your intelligence." They believed that being a gamer would make you antisocial and prone to violence. But what surprised me the most were the comments from the educational system. They were saying the same thing, and this would further fuel the notion that video games were bad for everyone.

The thought of having an Xbox 360 in the house concerned me a lot. I didn't know why, but I knew that the console was quickly becoming irresistible. The games had become faster, more intricate, and visually stunning. The graphics were mind blowing and the characters were funny. Keep in mind I still had no idea what I was looking at, but the picture was beautiful. I watched as my children set out to win each game and get better. All of a sudden, their circle of friends expanded in different directions. My children started playing with different gamers and different games. Arguing over whose turn it was to play and how long they were going to play became a constant battle. I found myself having to make a decision. Rather than listening to them argue, I purchased a second Xbox 360 and a new TV. Why? My children were doing extremely well in school and there was no reason for me to deny them.

The cost was starting to add up and I was frustrated with myself. Was I empowering this behavior? It's a PHASE, right?

Making a Deal with My Children

On the weekend, my house became a battlefield; my children had the ultimate control over everything. It was like watching a masterful gaming challenge that at some point, I was definitely going to lose. I believe I managed to have some control over the world of gaming, but I was missing something. We had to bring some type of resolution to the family, so we had a family meeting.

Our very first rule for the world of gaming was: You can only play on the weekend or when there is no school the next day. So, in other words, they could only play on Friday or Saturday. They could play when they were off from school the next day or when they were on school vacation or recess. But they would have to get their homework assignments done the first day. They could not play for hours at a time; there had to be breaks. There was no eating while playing.

The rules were in place, but they found a way to get around them, like children often do. I had to find a way to pull the reign back a little bit more, so I introduced an ingenious system. The children thought it was great at first too. It was simple and straightforward. For every perfect 100% on a test, they would earn 30 minutes of game time; for every 90%–99%, they would earn 15 minutes. My children laughed and said, "Oh, yes, this is great idea." In the back of my head, I was wondering why they agreed so easily. I knew this was going to go south. I did not know how fast!

As we started the grand master plan, it became clear that this system was flawed. It was a complete disaster. My children had accumulated so much time, they could play for the next year without breaking a sweat or taking a test. We had to hit the reset button and have another family meeting. I sat there, clueless. The master plan was completely out of my league when it came to video gaming and screen time. I was definitely treading through unmarked territory, and I had to find a balance.

We found ourselves caught up in something incredible. What were we going to do? How was I going to control this? My need to come up with a plan quickly was falling apart. I needed to take my time and develop something that was going to make an impact. It would have to benefit everyone. I changed the academic system to chores around the house. Now, this was going to be perfect! I would have a clean house, and they would get game time. Sunday through Thursday, they had daily chores to do, and they had to cross them off, when it was completed. When we got to Friday, we checked to make sure all the chores were done, and they were able to play. Maybe it did not benefit everyone, but it worked great for me.

Keeping Everything Balanced

Every day came with a new twist, and the children wanted to play more. We were uncertain about everything. Things were changing so fast, and we didn't have a clue. But it was through manipulation we found our greatest strength in balancing our children. We were not going to allow video games to take over our lives and consume our very souls.

We kept our children busy with all the activities they were involved in. We added trips and adventures. We took them out of the house and away from video games. We were keeping them balanced, and the schedule was tight and meticulous. I had the schedule for the Schedule.

Months into this plan, it became evident that our lives were in a state of disarray. What or who were we balancing? Did we involve our children in an unrealistic, overwhelming number of activities and events, forcing us to overlook our own imbalance? Each season came with its own set of challenges. We had a few activities that were yearly; but every season, they were involved in different traditional sports. We had completely lost ourselves in extra-curricular activities, we had to change clothes in the car. We even had dinner in the car in on the way to another activity.

The list of chores went out the window. They were so busy during the week that they did not have time to complete the list. This put the burden of keeping the house maintained on me and my husband; mostly on me because I had to make sure the proper uniforms were packed in the car with snacks, sneakers or cleats, and everything that went along with the activities of the day. Through all the chaos, I became unknowingly unbalanced.

Day in and day out, we continued this crazy schedule, and its demands put a strain on our physical being and our financial status. Traditional sports come at a high cost; they are not free. I had to keep them in sports to keep them off the gaming console. I was working so hard to not let them fall into the deep hole of video games, that I neglected to take care of my personal health. I was so tired. But as a mom, I always come last, and I just kept pressing on. I had to prove that "Wonder Woman" could do it all.

My children never complained about the relentlessly over-scheduled life. It just became our norm, and we embraced every new challenge.

The Negativity of Video Gaming

We talked about the negative aspects of video games; now I want to talk about my personal journey of challenging my perception and my thought patterns. Despite empowering my children and allowing them to indulge in playing video games, I still remain firm in believing that the games have an adverse effect on the mental well-being of gamers. It was a struggle to find concrete evidence or even find anything that would help me understand the impact of what was unfolding right before my eyes. I was feeling frustrated and confused because there were no studies that could help either way. Now, you can find anything thing. There are opinions and studies on both sides pendulum.

I relied on the opinion of educators and not the facts. When you think about it, I entrusted them with my children's academic education, so there was no reason why I shouldn't believe their views on video gaming. It should have some merit. To be honest, their concerns aligned with mine and it solidified my thoughts. In hindsight, this way of thinking put me at a disadvantage when it came to helping my children excel in the world of gaming, because their skills were getting better, and I did not know how to support them.

There was no way I could fully immerse myself in what was happening in the world of video gaming. I didn't understand the things my children were doing. I didn't know that they had transferable skills. I was trapped in this never-ending cycle, just like the movie *Groundhog Day*. I was filled with contradictory information and mixed emotions, and I simply could not embrace the concept of playing video games and how it could have a positive influence on my children's lives or anyone else's.

The internal struggle persisted and I wondered if this gaming thing would turn out to be just a waste of time. Were there any real opportunities to be found? When would this PHASE be over? Could I sell the consoles? What is the long-term objective in this uncharted territory?

Reflecting on my own indiscretions, I knew I wasn't going to engage with the games that were out there. There was no way I could play; they were too fast for me. At this time, I did not have the desire to try the games that were captivating the world. I was not interested. I'm sure I would have gotten better at some point but getting beaten by a 10- or 12-year-old definitely would have dampen my spirits.

Knowing what I know now there is one thing that parents have to do to help their gamers: Learn how to talk to your children about who they're playing with online. It's just like talking to them about their neighborhood and classroom friends. That's what I did, and it was a great way for me to connect with my children. I was able to get more insight on who they were playing with and what they were doing. I didn't know their real names—just the in-game name—but I was able to talk to my children about their gaming friends.

Converting the Room into a Gaming Room

We took on a new dimension, as parents of children that like to play video games. What did this mean? We decided that the stereotype about gamers was not true (at least not for our children), and we were not going to let it stop us from doing what we wanted to do for them. We did what any parent would do for their kids who like to play video games. We gave them a space for them to play. We transformed the extra bedroom into a gaming haven. We had no idea what we were getting into and how far it was going to go. I did not like where this road was taking me, but I continued on the journey. I was starting to get swallowed up in the world of gaming. I didn't like what it was making me do. I wanted to go back to Leapster, but we were way past Leapster and it was full steam ahead.

This room was perfect because it was right next to the kitchen. I spent most of my time in the kitchen and I could hear everything that was going on in the room. I didn't know the terminologies and I barely understood most of the things they were saying, but I could tell when they were upset, and I could ask about it. This room became their sanctuary, and they would invite their friends over for epic battles.

Let me tell you about this room. First, we put on a new coat of paint, and then it was time to get to work. Before you entered the room, the smell of freshly popped popcorn from the classic popcorn machine filled the air. As you walked into the room, you would immediately be attracted to the gumball machine, the candy machine, and the lighting that made you feel that you were in an arena. The glow in the room created the right mood to win battles and it made you feel like you were a pro. Next to the gumball machine was a stand that displayed different types of chips, corn puffs, cheese doodles, and pretzels. Standing next to the popcorn machine was a refrigerator that was stacked with different types of non-alcoholic beverages; this would make sure every gamer would not thirst for anything.

When you stepped into the room, you transformed into another euphoria. It was like a dystopian society; nothing else mattered. The gaming chairs were black and red and on the floor. There were two TV screens nestled perfectly on the wall for hours of gaming. Yes, I said hours. I don't know what had come over me lately. I was falling deep into this black hole.

We spared no expense when it came to the gaming room. Truth be told, I had no clue what I was doing. I just looked at some pictures and tried to copy them. I jumped through another hoop to help my children get through this phase.

The gaming room experience expanded way beyond their dreams, and that brought me nightmares. They were starting to engage with players from all over the globe, in different time zones. They were really starting to get the itch for playing video games and trying to stay up all night. They said sleeping was for the weak. I said they must be weak then, because they were going to get off and go to sleep.

Gaming continued to evolve, and it was starting to get into every nook and cranny of our lives. I did not like this, but I knew I had created it. I was starting to regret this every day; my children were engulfed and unable to resist playing one more game and having one more victory. I stood strong and did not let it take over, but conflicts started to begin. It was growing like weeds in the grass. Crazy things started to happen. My children's friends were getting kicked off Xbox because of their behavior. This did not stop them from playing. The kids would just change their in-game name and come back as someone new. The toxic behavior was out of control. I heard about fights that were happening in school because someone had lost a game online. I wanted my children to stop playing, but I couldn't tell them to get off because they were telling me what was happening. If I told them to get off because of what was happening, they would stop giving me the tea.

The information about toxic behavior and bullying left me mortified. Unfortunately, the young ladies seemed to get the worst of it. It broke my heart to hear what was happening. It was just a game, and you were just supposed to have fun. Why did they take it so seriously? Why were they so mad? It's just a game. It's not like they were a professional sport. Right? Neither one of my sons would scream, yell, or throw anything when they lost a game. They knew at a young age that you learn from your losses, and you get better. They would regroup, readjust, and work on their skills and get better.

I was hoping that I could shield them from the toxic players, but it was hard when I could not hear what the other player was saying. I quickly became the staff sergeant of the gaming room. I watched and I listened to their responses to other players. I could only imagine what the other players were saying.

At some point in time, my children moved up in rank and they were no longer playing with the poisonous players.

Chapter 3

Our First Grand Finals

Changing Consoles

Over the next few years, gaming consoles would transform, and so would I. The technology was incredible, and they were pushing boundaries. Consoles just kept surpassing their predecessor, with each new generation showing the world how innovative they were. It was at this time Xbox made a big leap from Xbox 360 to Xbox One. I was going to say it was a leap for me, but it wasn't—I was going to stay with my Xbox 360 and play *Just Dance*.

At the time of this announcement, I found myself completely behind the 8 ball, again. I had no idea there were other consoles. Who knew? Everyone but me. I had no idea there was a battle between Xbox and PlayStation to capture everyone's hearts and minds in the world of gaming. I don't know why my children played on Xbox instead of PlayStation. I guess it was because their friends were playing on Xbox. Whatever the reason, I didn't know the difference. I watched as parents around me became increasingly frustrated with the amount of time their children were playing on their consoles. I had no answers for them. I had no answers for me they didn't like because they would play. I just took the bull by the horns and let the chips fall where they may. The rules had to change when they had been on the console for too long, I would just tell them to get off. The longer they took to get off, the later they were able to get on the next day. They didn't like that because they would play with certain people in different time zones.

I didn't want to buy a new console, but I knew at some point I would break. What was I doing? Why couldn't I stop? When it came to making a purchase that was related to gaming, I felt like I had won a game. I guess it was my dopamine and I loved to see my children happy. But the financial aspects were wearing me down. I knew my children's friends would eventually buy the Xbox One and I would be pressured to do the same. I tried to get some of the parents to resist buying it, but that fell on deaf ears. No matter how much they did not like their children playing video games, they were going to make sure their kids had the newest console to play on.

There was not much that I could say. After all, I had empowered this behavior for years. I don't even know why I contemplated this situation, because eventually, you know I would buy them.

Here we are, a happy family of two brand new Xbox One consoles. Hoping it was a Phase was not working.

I Want to Go to the Grand Finals

My grandmother used to say that time waits for no man and time was flying. The past few years felt like moments in time instead of years. We were zooming and bustling along. Gaming was smooth (I guess) and we had no obstacles in sight. I reluctantly admit I didn't research anything about the gaming world; I was still just going with the flow, trying to piece things together on my own.

Spring 2018 brought a curveball to my world. My children were excited, and they were walking around the house talking about how they were going to an event, and it was going to be amazing. Get ready everyone, because they wanted to go to a gaming event—some kind of showdown, I think. It was called the Overwatch League Grand Finals, and it was going to be at the Barclays Center in New York City. Well, this was very close to us! What are the odds? Can you believe it? This virtual haven decided to leap off the screen and into a real-life building. What kind of fairy tale was this? I was comfortable at my level of knowledge, and a new twist was crashing down on me! This event threw me for a loop, and it left me breathless.

Naturally, I had to ask about the event and what to expect. Both of them started talking at once, trying to tell me what was going to happen. They were talking faster and faster. I had to stop them and tell them to slow down so that I could understand. "Take a breath, guys," I said. They started to explain it to me slowly.

Well, this is what I got out of it. It was called an Esports event and it would last for two days. Now we were no longer video gamers. We have Esports players. They went on to say that the best players in the league would come together to compete for a lot of money. Let me stop here. I didn't know there was a league. Was it a league like the Avengers? After all, they were on the screen and not real. They rolled their eyes and tried to explain it to me. They said, "It is a league like regular sports; like your favorite football or baseball team."

No matter how hard they tried, the pieces simply refused to fall into place. I tried to make a connection, but I could not. "OK, tell me more about this Esports thing and how it is different from playing a video game." My oldest son said, "Oh, come on, Ma, really? Esports is competitive players that come together to compete while playing video games." "Oh," I said. "I get it." No, I didn't. I saw players competing online. So, what made this different?

My children continued to explain: "The players compete online and in person through brackets, and the final teams make it to the grand finals, like the Superbowl or the World Series."

OK, now they were talking my language, and I got it. It's just like traditional sports. But do they seed them the same? A question for another day.

"So, there are professionals in the world of Esports?"

"Yes, Ma!"

"Now, tell me why you want to go to the event. You can watch the same thing on YouTube or Twitch for free."

"Ma, it's for the excitement."

"Really? How exciting could it be to watch someone play video games? This makes no sense."

My head was spinning but they were finally able to Bridge the Gap between my confusion and the gaming universe. I was curious despite the fact I didn't understand. How serious could this competition be?

It became abundantly clear how bad they wanted to go. So, I did what any parent would do, who doesn't like gaming. I caved in and said I was going to buy the tickets.

Finding Tickets

For days on end, my children wouldn't stop rambling about the big event. It was as if they were seasoned veterans, bragging about their past experience. They have never been to an in-person Esports professional tournament. They have only seen it on YouTube or Twitch.

I work my tail off for every penny I earn, so the idea of spending my hard-earned cash on something I couldn't quite wrap my head around, sounded crazy. Wait a minute. I was turning into my parents. The very thought made me quiver! Why do we morph into our parents as we get older?

In the background, I could hear my children rambling. I felt like Princess Peach, looking for someone like Donkey Kong to swoop in and rescue me from this relentless babbling. OK, that's the extent of my gaming jargon.

The tickets were not on sale yet, and the pressure to buy them was building. I could see that the ticket buying process was going to be difficult. You had to be fast or they would sell out. The day to buy tickets was getting closer. My children's excitement rocketed to new heights, making time feel like it was standing still.

The moment was finally here—time to buy the tickets. Everyone gathered around my computer; they huddled like a team trying to make a play for a touchdown. I could feel my children's breath, making the hairs on the back of my neck stand on end. I told them to move back; they were making me nervous.

They were steadily looking at the screen, and both of them, at the same time, pointed and said, "There they are! Let's get them. Hurry before they sell out!" I clicked on them and that's when another choice showed up: general admission or general admission with the master package—the dreaded question. Which one were we going to get? My sanity depended upon it. I asked my children which ones they wanted, but all they did was look at each other and shrug their shoulders, stating that they didn't know. There was an awkward silence, so I took my finger and pressed on master package tickets. If I had to go, it might as well be In-Style.

The countdown began ticking away. I glanced at the remaining time, and I felt I had enough time to complete the transaction. With the children so close to me, the pressure was building. I inadvertently put in the wrong credit card numbers, and guess what? We ran out of time—back to the beginning. I was not going to let this shake my confidence. I pressed the purchase button once again, watching the timer reset. We timed out again. I looked at them and said, "Third time's a charm or we can kiss the tickets goodbye." I laid down the law, ordering silence—no giggling, no groans, no bodily noises—just stillness or they would have to leave the room.

Finally, I was able to enter the correct numbers from my credit card and all the information in time. I printed out the precious tickets and put them in a safe place. I could hear my children talking in the distance, saying, "She ordered four tickets; who are we going to take with us?"

Telling My Underage Children That They Were Not Going Alone

There's nothing better than being a parent. It is truly a test of your patience. My children really thought they were going to go to the Barclay Center without me and their dad. You have got to be kidding me. Unbelievable! Children of law enforcement officers, venturing out alone in the Big Apple—not happening. There was no way I was going to let them hop on the train to Brooklyn without adult supervision.

Here we go. I tried to navigate through this situation with flare. But through the pandemonium, I knew I had to bring some humor to the table. We gathered around the dining table to have lunch and we were laughing at the daily events as we often do. All of a sudden, my children started to talk about who they wanted to take to the event, and they were very excited about it. In my infinite wisdom, I stated, "Why don't you just take your father and me?" Their eyes met and they started to laugh. I did not say anything funny, I was serious.

"Oh, you guys have no idea what's going on," they said, shaking their heads.

Well, I playfully interrupted and said, "Well, this would be a great opportunity for us to learn all about video games."

They once again broke out into laughter. They continued to find this funny, and I became irritated. I stood up from the table and started to clear it. I said, "Neither one of you will be going anywhere without me and your father." The laughter silenced and their faces became very grim, and they looked a little frustrated.

"What do you mean you're going?" they protested.

I took in a deep breath and exhaled slowly, and stated, "It's not that I don't trust you. I don't trust the other people.

I finished cleaning the table and went into the kitchen. I couldn't help but overhear their conversation. I am always listening.

"How bad could it really be if we went with them?" one of them said. "But we're old enough to go on our own," the other one chimed in. "Let's think about this. If they come along, we won't have to pay for anything. They will buy us everything we want!" They both paused and then the approval came. "Hmm, I guess you have a point." One said.

Moments later, they marched into the kitchen, wearing sneaky grins, and they said in unison, "All right, we talked it over; we're going to let you come with us!" I could not contain my laughter. They were actually granting me and their father permission to go with them to the event. It was hilarious, and all I could do was laugh, realizing that sometimes you have to just embrace the win, no matter how you get it. I was excited to go.

Just when you thought the excitement couldn't get any better, they dropped another bombshell. They announced that DJ Khaled was going to be at the event! My jaw dropped and my anticipation for the event went to new heights!

I was excited about going, especially after I was given permission.

Preparing for a Tournament I Didn't Understand

As the day grew nearer, my house became a whirlwind of excitement. I didn't know it at the time, but Esports had become an unstoppable phenomenon, winning over the hearts of millions, globally. I found myself having difficulties with this unfamiliar territory, and I was honestly trying to navigate through this accelerating world.

I was determined to enjoy the day. As I was preparing for the event, my inner nerd said, "Bring a book. I am sure you will have time to read on the train and at the event." After all, they were just playing a video game.

I realized that there was a distinct difference between Esports players and the gamers. Maybe I was starting to Bridge the Gap in my mind and develop a deeper connection with the world of Esports.

I took a few minutes to look at the train schedule, and I saw that our route would require a transfer at Jamaica Ave. station. It had been a decade since my last train ride, and I was embracing the chance to relax on the train. There were a multitude of departure times from my station, and I had to make sure we arrived at the transfer station without a long wait because The Jamaica Ave. station has always been an experience, with the bustling of hundreds of people and the battling of the gusty wind that penetrates one's core. But it was July and there shouldn't be any wind. I guess we would find out.

Friday, May 18, 2018, had arrived. We made our way to the train station and took a short walk to the escalator, which carried us up to the platform, making this the beginning of what would change my outlook. A few minutes later, the train pulled into the station, and we got onto a packed train with not one seat in sight. Well, there was no reading for me at this point. I wanted to know where everybody was going. It was a Friday, and we were going in the opposite direction of the workforce.

We made it to the Jamaica Ave. station, and without any delay everyone got off the train and stood on the platform for the connecting Atlantic terminal train. Moments later, the train bound for Atlantic Ave. approached Jamaica Ave. station. The crowd got closer to the platform edge and, all at once, everyone boarded the train. It is New York and you have to move with the crowd or be left behind. I was able to get a seat, but the ride was going to be so short, there would be no time to read my book.

The train reached the Atlantic terminal stop and every passenger left the train. It was the last stop. But then everyone walked across the street to the Barclay Center, and that was when it all changed.

Entering the Barclay Center

We crossed the street and as we got closer to the entrance doors, I felt like I was at Comic Con. I am an avid Marvel enthusiast and I do know about Comic Con, but this was totally different. Everyone either had on their favorite character costume or their favorite team's jersey, except for me and my husband. We were out of place but we were ready for the adventure.

We walked to the main entrance, and the staff directed us to the master package entrance to the right. We followed the directions of the staff member, but we must have walked past it. Did he mean his right or our right?

When we got to the back of the Barclay Center and asked the staff member, he said the other guy pointed us in the wrong direction. We finally made it to the master package entrance. We walked in with great anticipation, handed over our tickets, and they handed us our merch bag. It had the regular stuff in it: lanyards, towels, pamphlets, and giveaways from sponsors. The music was pulsating, and I couldn't wait to get inside. We walked up a few steps to get into the building and I could taste the energy that was coming from inside. I watched as people walked by in extravagant costumes, laughing and having a great time. I think I was more excited than my children were at this point.

The music was pumping, and everyone was trying to buy new merch. People were trying to find their friends, who were once behind them but no longer there. I think everyone was taken in by the whirlwind and the energy that was going on and got distracted. The atmosphere ignited every sense of my being. The excitement of everyone around me generated my curiosity. I wanted to see what was going on inside. That was when I realized this was bigger than anything I could have imagined. This was something I had to see in person. It was going to be a part of history. I understood why my children wanted to be here.

We walked into the arena, and I was consumed by the energy. The crowd was really loud. We walked through the aisle and found our seats. I began to survey our surroundings; looking for exit signs, but the one thing that stood out was the ages of the people that were in the audience. I looked at my children and said, "Take a good look at all the people in this arena. These are the people you are playing with online. This is why I tell you to be careful. They are a lot older than you are."

There was so much going on, I didn't know what to focus on, so I sat back and took out my book. Yes, I took out my book, with all that energy around me. But then they announced DJ Khaled. The crowd went wild, and I didn't think that it could get any louder, but it did. Let's just say I put the book back in my bag. It was infectious, and the crowd was intoxicating. I put my bag on my seat, and I did what every parent loves to do: I embarrassed my children. The pulsating music called me out and I was dancing. Yes, I was dancing and having a blast. Let's be clear, no matter what my children say, I can dance. I come from a dancing family with several professional dancers, so I can dance. I had to keep up with the rest of the family. I allowed myself to be in the moment and enjoy every bit of it. I had stepped into the world of Esports, and I loved it.

The Adrenaline Rush

The moment we had been waiting for started; they began announcing the teams, and this experience transcended me to another realm. As each player made their way onto the stage, a deafening roar erupted from the crowd. I had never been to an event with so much vitality. With each passing moment, I got more excited.

The audience was chanting. It was so intense; they drew me into everything that was going on. I could not deny the thrill it gave me and how it made me feel. Maybe this was what my children were feeling when they were playing video games.

I was no longer that parent that didn't know anything, or at least I didn't look like it, because I stood there clapping when the audience clapped, and I screamed when the audience screamed. What was I clapping and screaming at? I didn't know. I was just going with the moment and having fun.

Day one came to a close and I was exhausted. The rush to the train, with all of the spectators, was ferocious. We ran to the car at the front train, and we were able to get seats. Everyone on the train was talking about the event. My heart was still racing; I really enjoyed it.

We arrived at Jamaica Ave. station, but as we stood on the platform that was crowded with Overwatch enthusiasts, we listened as they were still cheering on their favorite team. We talked about the event all the way home. The boys talked us into buying them some new merch. We knew that was a plan from the beginning. My children were excited about tomorrow and I have to admit, I was too.

On the second day of the Overwatch Grand Finals, we followed the same routine, but this time I made a conscious decision to leave my book at home. I wanted to have fun and embarrass my children, once again.

As the game began, I had a better understanding of what was supposed to happen. Humm... You have to get the tank across the line. That's it! Okay, I was simplifying it—you do have to endure a couple of battles to get the tank across the line. Now, I know why so much time is devoted to playing the game. In the end, London Spitfire proved that at this tournament they were the best, and they became the champions of the Overwatch Grand Finals 2018.

This was a learning moment for me. Sometimes you have to listen to your children. They may teach you something new.

THE FIRST FINALS
OVERWATCH LEAGUE
GRAND FINALS
NYC 2018
CAPTURE HISTORY
JULY 27 & 28

Chapter 4

The Pushback

Letting Go

A few days after the Overwatch Grand Finals, my son decided that he no longer needed his Xbox, and he was moving on to a PC. That is what the professional players were using, and if he wanted to be a professional player, he had to play on a PC. I do not know what took him so long to ask me. I knew this was coming. It was in his best interest to ask me while I was still on fire from the OGF.

I looked at the prices for gaming PCs, and it was ridiculous. "Are you out of your mind?" Mommy's ATM card was going on strike. I'd had enough.

"Don't worry about it; I'm going to build my own PC," he said.

"Don't worry," he said. I still had to buy the parts. I had no idea he knew how to build a PC. Maybe he learned how to do it in the Robotics clubok.

He went on Amazon and picked out the items he needed to build the PC. Again, I was enabling this behavior. A few days later, he received all the parts and started to work on the PC. He was in his room for a couple of hours when he texted me—yes, texted me. Why come downstairs and talk to me?

He was having trouble getting the PC to start. So, I climbed up the stairs and walked into his room that had boxes and bubble wrap all over the place. I asked him what was wrong, and he told me that it would not start. I really didn't hear anything else. All I heard was, "Wah! Wah! Wah!" I wanted to break down the boxes and get the garbage bag for the rest of the stuff. I snapped out of it and said, "Let's just go to the Geek Squad and have them look at it."

After a few moments with them looking at the PC, the Geek Squad said, "All you have to do is lift this and put this screw in here and it will work. You did a great job putting the PC together by yourself—do you want a job?" He laughed but I thought it was a good idea—get a job and get off that computer, because you can't get a job with video games.

We conquered another hurdle, and he was on his way to learning how to play video games on a PC. It only took his brother a day to ask him to build a computer for him. What was going on? What happened to playing on the console? Where was this going to take us? How many levels are left? Everyone said it was just a phase—when was this phase going to end? Looking back - All I did was stand in the shadows and pay for everything. What was going to happen with the gaming room? How was I going to hear the tea?

It was in January of 2019 when my oldest son came to me and said, "Ma, you have to let him go. You have to let him play more. He is really good." I replied that I understood what he was saying but that I wasn't ready for this. He said, "Ma, no, you don't understand."

"You're right, I don't."

"Ma, really, he is good and he's not playing with the toxic people. He's moving up and he is on a different level. He is a Grandmaster."

"What does that mean?"

"He is one of the best in the world."

"The world! By world, do you mean the United States?"

"No, the world!"

How could this be? How big is Esports? How much more will have to endure? I thought I was done. I didn't know how much more of this I could take. I took one step forward and was pushed back two steps. This was a difficult decision for me to make. But by now, you know me—I gave in after a few days. I lifted the restrictions, and I didn't know the slippery slope I was unleashing.

Contenders

My household underwent a shift, with both of my children moving their gaming skills out of the game room and into their bedrooms. The once vibrant bustling room was now quiet. Everything I had created was worthless. How could they just move on? They suggested that I get rid of the Xbox One, but I said no. I could use it to play Just Dance.

I lifted the restrictions, but there was one restriction that was not going to be lifted. They had to maintain a 4.0 GPA or the gaming world as they knew it would end. I allowed them to reduce some of their activities while still remaining active in Science Olympiad, Tri M, Deca, HOBY, National Honor Society, Tennis, and the Award winning Competitive Marching Band. The marching band was seasonal and it required a lot of dedication. I really enjoyed watching them perform on the field.

My younger son started joining Esports teams and competing with players with the same mindset. I started to see that this may not be a phase. He was learning and growing from his experience. He was playing on Twitch. What is Twitch? It is a spin off from Justin.tv and it is a great streaming source for gamers. You can see competitions in real time.

As far as Esports contenders go—I'm going to talk from experience and not as the mom that did not understand—every game title has their own name for a player's journey to pro. Overwatch contenders just happen to be ours. Contenders is a series of exciting competitions that captures millions of people globally. They have brackets and are seeded. I was starting to understand his journey; it was like traditional sports. I would track his team's progress every week. Did I know what I was looking at? No! But I found myself enjoying the quest I was thrown into. The competitors were impressive, and I was a mom learning how to appreciate the dedication behind the game.

My son's dedication to improving his skills was clear and he was going through contenders' tiers effortlessly; but for him, it might have felt like eternity. I started to learn the names of the teams and the In-game names of the players. My son surrounded himself with great friends. Who thought you could have a social life as a gamer? I did! That is the one thing, I saw that from the beginning. I watched my son and his friends evolve together and transform their hobby into a passion called Esports, and I knew that he was going to go far in this untraditional sport.

Trying to Get the School District to Understand

In the spring of 2019, my excitement for the world of Esports grew. I was not an expert, but I was no longer a noob (newbie), and I could see the advantages of having a team in our local high school. I started to dive deeper into the competitive world of Esports. My son was playing online, and he started to make a name for himself. Since he really understood the world of Esports, I thought we should introduce the idea of having a high school team to the district.

I started to look up Esports in high school and I came across two educational programs. I researched both of the programs and I liked the concept, but I didn't know how we were going to implement them. One of the programs had a map that showed how many schools had an Esports program. Esports was big in the middle of the country. I could not believe how this was growing in the United States, and we knew nothing about it on the East Coast. Okay, I knew nothing about it.

I have always been hungry for knowledge and introducing new programs in our school's district and local clubs was my forte. I have always been involved in empowering our youth and I saw how this could help our high school students or even our middle school students. It had great potential, and it could keep them excited about going to school. I decided to propose an Esports program to the district. I went to a meeting, and I was armed with all the material I needed. I was determined to get them to say yes, but I was given an ill-advised no. It was more like, "You got to be kidding me." They were stuck on the gaming aspect, not the transferable skills or educational value I was trying to explain to them. I was not used to getting a no. My proposals were always approved. Maybe I wasn't prepared. Maybe they were not prepared. This was heartbreaking; this program was going to change everything.

I watched as the Esports programs started to grow in other nearby districts—how could they let this happen? My district was always on the cutting edge and a trendsetter. Listen to yourself, lady. Get it together. This was just a stumble, so don't give up. Channeling my inner self, I continued the conversation, and they continued to say no. I could not believe they were so closed-minded. I knew they thought it was a phase, like I once did. How was I going to get the district on board?

I was determined to get a team. Any and every chance I had, I would talk about Esports. I was trying to wear them down. I was relentless. I would text and e-mail them about Esports all the time. They were not interested and wanted nothing to do with it. I was not going to stop; it was my mission. Countless students were depending on me to introduce this to the district. I would have to reframe my approach and come back a different way.

The Vacation

We have gone on countless vacations throughout the years. We even want on another cruise, but it was not during hurricane season. The time had come to take another gr at adventure together. Where should we go? Of course, I said we can always go to Disney. But I was ruled out; they wanted to go someplace else. They felt they were too old to go to Disney. I quickly said "No one is ever too old to go to Disney." I have gone to Disney World since I was a little girl and I still get excited when I think about going there.

I don't remember who it was, but somebody said, "What about a cruise from Spain?" That piqued my curiosity, so I started to look for cruise lines leaving from Spain. Everyone was thrilled about going on another cruise. I found some exciting excursions; I was ready to go. But when I was about to—you guessed it—hit that button, I could hear my husband in the background talking with the children. Well, they were not children anymore. They were young men.

"Maybe we should go to Hawaii?" my older son said. I could hear them laughing and getting excited. Here we go again! All the plans I made were all about to change, again.

I walked out of the office and looked at all three of them and said, "Well, what are we going to do?"

Without hesitation, they all said, "Hawaii." That was when my younger son said, "How long are we going to be there? I have competitions." He had never asked this question before, so I guess Esports was really serious. I replied, "It's Hawaii; you can't stay less than seven days." With a look of sadness on his face, he walked away, because he had to tell his team he would not be around for seven days. My heart grew weary because I didn't want him to miss out on what he loved. But I was not going to let this Esports thing ruin our family's vacation.

I went back into the office, canceled everything for the cruise, and started looking for places to stay in Hawaii. I decided we would go in July, and we could celebrate everything. We would have birthdays, graduations, and anniversaries to commemorate, and I knew the perfect place we could stay: Alani, of course. This Disney girl was going get her Disney fix, no matter what!

Our journey to Hawaii was going to be a long one, and there was one connecting flight each way. I had no idea if my young men were going to survive without their gaming systems. I'm sure there were some type of withdrawals, but they never complained. Once we set foot on that beautiful, exquisite island. We became a part of the culture, I knew they were not thinking about Esports—at least I hoped they weren't.

The next morning, with a severe case of jet lag, we got up before the sun rose and walked out into the open field near the hotel, where we found several like-minded people waiting for the sun to rise over the mountain. As we stood in anticipation of the sun, we watched as it slowly rose over the mountain top. It was magnificent; I had never seen a sunrise that beautiful in my life. I felt like I could touch the heavens. No sunrise will ever impact me the same.

Thankfully my young men did not have time to think about Esports—every day was full of excitement. We went to luaus, the Cultural Center, and several historic places, which is a must for everyone. The Alani Hotel treated us like royalty, and the beach was paradise.

We swam in the crystal -clear water of Hawaii was surprised when a sea lion swam past us. I will never forget that moment. I could not move. I was frozen in time.

Hawaii ended up being my family's favorite vacation. This Disney girl ended up making everyone's dreams come true in this magical paradise.

When the World Changed

It had been a while since I thought about the district and the esports proposal. I had been meandering on how to execute it. But as November of 2019 rolled in. I had an epiphany. I was doing it all wrong. My past attempts were a big flop and not what they were looking for. I realized it wasn't me they wanted to hear from but a student. Hmm... They rarely said no to a student. I liked what I was about to throw down. I told my son to write the e-mail to the district and tell them about Esports and how he feels about it, also make sure to tell them he had been practicing with the local collegiate Varsity Esports team. He wrote a quick e-mail, and in less than 24 hours, he got a response. The district asked him to do a presentation at the January 2020 school board meeting. This was good, really good. We were just one presentation away from creating a team. It was going to happen.

My son put together a quick PowerPoint presentation, sent it to the district for approval, and he was ready and so was I. However, as January got closer, we found ourselves in a dilemma. I had two events scheduled for the same night. How the heck did this happen? My schedules are tight and on point all the time. But we had to make a choice. What was more important? We chose to go to another event and postponed the presentation to the board. It was rescheduled for March 2020. I know you can see where this is going.

As we entered into the month of March, I watched as the world slowly transformed. With every passing day, I knew that our family needed to be together and our college man had to come home. I told my husband that we would have to pick up our son from college because I wanted him home. Well, Mr. Let's-Wait-It-Out agreed and everything around was starting to close down. I was happy when my son arrived home and the entire family was together. In just a few days after my son was home, the world as we knew it completely shut down.

Needless to say, the presentation was canceled indefinitely.

The world continued to evolve as we all tried to make sense of what was happening. I was trying to adjust our lifestyles to make it through this world changing event. We could not go anywhere or do anything. What were we going to do? As for me, I prayed, and I went from one church to the other on YouTube. That is when I found my church, "Elevation," in Charlotte, North Carolina. Pastor Steven Furtick spoke the truth and it helped me get through the pandemic. I have not missed a Sunday sermon since then.

Not everyone was looking for a divine intervention to get through the pandemic. Most people found something they liked to do. Some people started online businesses; some people started to DJ on Instagram. My neighborhood had wine fairies. People would unanimously drop off wine at other people's houses. They did not just drop off a bottle; it was perfectly crafted and decorated. I don't remember who started it or how it started, but it gave a lot of joy to people who were not able to get out of their houses.

With everything closing around there was one thing that stayed active. It was the gamers. They dove into gaming, and they created new avenues to communicate with each other while improving their skills. Gaming was becoming the new safe haven for everyone to escape and have some type of normalcy. The gaming world exploded, and it seemed like everybody was taking on new challenges in the world of Esports.

I would not see my children for hours. They said they were in class and would only emerge when it was their scheduled lunchtime, and in the evening for dinner. This was getting out of control. I had to take matters into my own hands and plan family time. My children expressed their disapproval of the new activities that were going to unfold. They said: "Why does she always have to do something?" I said, "Because that is what I do."

After going down this path with my children for a few days, they finally came around and started to have fun. We pressed through the pandemic together and shifted our priorities. My son never got a chance to give his presentation to the school board.

Getting Better

Every day, my son got better at his craft, but what was he striving for? What was the end game? I still had no idea what was happening, but with each passing moment, I was looking for the next level that I had to conquer. The moments flew by so fast, I could not remember what day it was. The weeks become a blur.

I was sitting in the dining room watching Michael Simon do his daily recipe show, when my son handed me a stack of papers. I guess I was supposed to know what this was. "What is this, and what are you doing now?" Get ready; here we go! The look on his face scared me. He was so happy.

"Ma, I have been asked to be on a highly competitive contender's team."

"Wait a minute; I thought you were already on the contender's team."

"Yes and no! Can you please sign the contract? I have to send it back. This is a great opportunity for me to have fun while showcasing my skills, and I can win money."

Now he had my attention. "Win money? How do you do that?"

"We will compete in tournaments for prize pools."

Every time I conquer a level, a new one appeared. I knew the pros won money, but when did everybody else start winning money? I was going to have to do some research. He went on to say, "I have been competing in small scholarship tournaments and winning. But contenders are different, and since I am under 18, you have to give me permission to play."

I could not let him down, so without hesitation, I signed the contract. My mind was racing to keep up with what he was saying. Little did I know that this decision was going to put me deeper into the world of Esports. There was no time to breathe, no time to assess what was happening, and I was just moving faster with every changing moment.

How was I going to get ahead of this thing? How was I going to get control of this?

I started to see some of the intricacies of Esports, but this field demanded dedication and discipline to excel. The gaming circuit was more complex than I thought. Now he had coaches and managers helping him to improve his skills. They were critiquing games so that the team could get better. This was really starting to sound like traditional sports.

Still Not Understanding

When I look back and see how I was easily manipulated, and how innocent everything was as it gently guided me into this phenomenal world known as Esports. I had no idea what was going on. Who could have foreseen this? It was really a secret society waiting to be uncovered, waiting to be explored and mastered by me, with every twist and turn leading me down the path to another winding road.

I wanted to know more, but where would I start? Who would I talk to? My friends had no clue. They just let their kids play and knew nothing about the game or the people they were playing with. They wanted nothing to do with this Esports thing. But yet, they continued to fight with their children about how many hours they were playing on their console, and how they would become violent when they lost a game. Yes, their children were still playing on consoles while mine were on PCs. So, I guess there really wasn't anything we could talk about. But then again, maybe we could talk about their children's reactions when they lose a game. My children didn't act that way. I started to feel sorry for my friends because they had no idea what they were missing out on. Neither did I, but I was more in tune with my children, and I could have a conversation with them about gaming.

I thought about playing Overwatch to get more insight, but that thought quickly dissipated. I didn't want to play that game. It was too advanced for me; I could not understand the strategy or what the end game was. I knew it was to win, but how was I going to do that? I could not excel in the battles.

I was stuck in the middle of a world I needed to master. I had to become more than an outsider. I wanted to get into the club; I wanted to be a part of the team. But more importantly, I had to get out of the confusion and transform into a mom that knows everything about Esports.

My children were enjoying Esports, and I was honestly tired of feeling like there was no end. I wanted to get ahead of it. I had to find a way to become victorious. Where could I get the information and what was the best way to support my children? The path ahead would be treacherous, but I had been able to conquer every hurdle so far, and I was up for the challenge.

I started to ask my children more questions and, of course, they were irritated at first, but I asked them to be patient with me. I just wanted to be a part of the world they were in, and in order for me to do that, I would have to ask a lot of questions.

Chapter 5

The Search for a College

What Are We Looking For?

We made it to the end of junior year with a 4.0 GPA, and he was happy. We were all happy. He was able to maintain a 4.0 GPA after being thrown into an everchanging world of Esports and the pandemic. As we prepared for senior year, the search for college, and what he was going to do in Esports, began. Throughout the summer, I pushed and pushed my son to look for schools to apply to. But contenders got in the way.

He was still trying to figure out his major, but when you add Esports to the search, it becomes a whole new challenge. I thought this was going to be easy. "Why not apply to the same schools as your brother?" I suggested. "At least we were able to visit those schools before the pandemic." He said, "No. We are looking for a school that has a Varsity Esports team and my major."

New levels, new challenges... here we go again. At least this time I was not completely ambiguous about Esports in college. He had played with a Varsity Esports team at one of our local college and they offered him $500 to play on their team. I assumed that all the colleges had scholarships for Esports players. I would quickly learn that was not true.

September rolled in like a banshee, and I now had a high school senior who had not decided on what college to apply to. I was frustrated but determined to make him sit down and figure out where he was going to apply. I gave him a week to figure it out.

I wanted all applications to be submitted by November 1, 2020. I did that with my oldest son and by Thanksgiving, we were receiving acceptance letters. He agreed with my plan and we started the college process: FAFSA, Common app, and essay's

One good thing about applying to several schools at this time was, we didn't have to worry about application fees. Also, several of the schools did not require a SAT or ACT test score, because test sites were shut down. I thought to myself, he will be able to pick any school and apply for free. What is better than that?

Google Search

Whenever you're looking for something online, the go-to place is Google. So, Google gave me the top colleges/universities that have an Esports program. It gave me 10 results. The schools were either in the middle of the country or further West. This would require a plane ride and I did not feel comfortable with that. What would I do if there was an emergency? We were still in a pandemic. Would I drive 12–15 hours or take a plane? Of course, I would, but I would rather have him closer to home.

We kept researching and kept asking the question in different ways, but the same top ten schools kept coming up. Were they the only schools with Esports? No, that could not be. After all, my son was practicing with the local college, so there had to be more out there. What keywords were we missing? There had to be something that we were forgetting. We searched and we searched, looking for something close, but I could see by the look on his face that he wanted to go to a school that was far away... like California!

I was tired and I had tried several different ways, but the same schools keep coming up. Maybe the information wasn't online yet. Maybe the information was only for the "secret society." I looked at the colleges that were coming up, and I was about to throw in the towel when I said to myself, "You cannot do this like your other child. This is not the same."

I decided to look for professional help. I found an Esports recruiter, and they had more than 10 college/universities with an Esports program. Yes, it was going to cost money, but I needed the help, and time was ticking. I didn't know what else to do. I guess Mommy's ATM was open for business again.

I signed my son up with a recruitment program and made a list of the colleges that were on the website and I started to research. We were able to come up with at least 25 schools that had his major and a Varsity Esports program. Some schools even had Esports as a major. After further diving into the collegiate scene, we found out that it was a business degree, but many of the classes were centered around management in the Esports industry.

My son filled out several interest forms online and he was headed in the right direction. Not every school had an online interest form or a way to contact the Esports program. We found ourselves in a dilemma when it came to finding an e-mail, so we contacted them through the recruitment website. To this day, finding information for coaches or directors for some schools is still challenging. You have to find them on Discord, IG, or Twitter aka X.

We were flooded with e-mails from coaches trying to reach out to him for their Varsity team. Clearly, this was a good idea. Many schools had blanket e-mails, but we knew how to weed those out. Keeping up with the coaches' names and schools was an easy task once we created a spreadsheet.

All applications were in by November 1st, 2020, and all we had to do was sit back and wait.

** As I am writing this book, I decided to google the top Esports colleges/universities. Some of the same school came up. **

Interviews With Coaches

On November 15, 2020, college acceptance e-mails started to roll in. By Christmas, he had been accepted to more than half of the schools. Some of the schools were so creative with their acceptance packages. I was really impressed with all the merch they sent. As each acceptance came in, he put their banner on the wall in the game room. Yes, it was still the game room. I hadn't decided what I was going to do with the room yet. I knew he would be accepted to all of the schools. There was no doubt in my mind. His resume and transcript were outstanding. It had been hard to keep up with all the activities in the past, but it was worth it, and it was great for his applications; especially for one of the schools in California. They wanted a well-rounded student, and they had a holistic approach to accepting students into their school. This school was so popular that they reported 107,000 students applied for the fall of 2021. They only accepted 32,528, and—you guessed it—he was one of the 32,528 that got in. You know my dilemma with this. It was time to talk to the Esports coaches and directors, so we could get a better look at the schools.

The interview process was interesting because everything was still online. I had no doubt in my mind that he would surpass the expectations of the coach during the recruitment process. There was so much to do, and time was going by quickly. Somehow, I became his secretary, weeding out the e-mails that were phishing and making sure he maintained a 4.0 GPA.

We had to make another spreadsheet to make sure the interviews did not overlap. We had 30 minutes in between interviews in case they were late, or the interview ran overtime. If you recall, I have mentioned Discord before. Discord is a popular streaming app that coaches/directors use to conduct interviews. I would advise everyone to get a Discord account. Parent should monitor the account.

He created an introduction page for his interviews. This would allow him to have key answers at his fingertips:

- GPA
- School clubs
- Outside of school activities

- Volunteer work
- What he likes about that college
- Names of some of the players on the team
- His current stats for his game
- Upcoming games

A lot, if not most, of the schools with Esports were going through a growth period. Many of the school had only been established two years and they were still trying to find their way. The coaches would interview and recruit the students, but it was the director who got the students to commit to the program.

We learned how to navigate through this process and dominate the interview. The first interviews set a precedence for interviews that would follow. We learned what to do quickly.

In the process I found out that there were some questions more important than others. Here are two:

- Does your school allow the player to keep the winnings from a game or tournament, or does your school keep the winnings to sustain the program?
- Do you have a Varsity Esports team or club?

There was one school that said they had a Varsity Esports team, but everybody plays.

I can hear you laughing from here. I was still learning, but I wasn't new. I knew this was totally wrong. Why would everyone play? I knew the difference between an Esports Varsity team and a club. Why wouldn't they want their best players compete?

We were not playing little league baseball, with the coach being a dad and everyone gets a participation trophy. This is college Esports, which is like traditional sports, where every school wants great players, or good players that they can make great. This was not the place for my son. I was disappointed because this school was just one state over. Maybe I had to start accepting the fact that he would attend a school that was farther away. Nah!

Establishing the Tempo

After three or four interviews, I could see which direction this was going. There was a tempo, a certain type of rhythm, that I was feeling with each conversation. I was impressed with all the passion every coach had for their program.

Here are 10 basic questions out of the 26 we created to ask a coach or director.

1. What is the minimum GPA required to remain on the team?
2. Do your players graduate in four or five years?
3. Is it possible to join other activities?
4. Are your tryouts before or after committing to your school?
5. What rank are you looking for?
6. When are the practices and competitions?
7. What positions are you looking for?
8. What kind of player are you looking for?
9. What happens to the money that is won in tournaments?
10. What is my final out-of-pocket cost?

Sometimes they had a question we did not anticipate. In that instance, I would write a rebuttal question down on the index card and slide it to my son to ask. The coaches always wanted the family present. After the initial intro I would sit on the side or behind the computer. It was his interview, and I was the coaches to see his magic. No matter where I was, I wrote down every single answer the coach/director gave. There was a case where one school that did not invite family to the interview. Little did they know, I was there all the time.

Make sure your child is prepared for the interview. Interviews can consist of several people from the university. They review all of the activities my son participated in at high school and discussed how those same activities were on their college campus. They also discussed scholarship options if he joined the same clubs on their campus. They offered him great packages.

If you have an Esports player that is looking to get into college, don't let them stop their extracurricular activities. Sometimes people look for only one scholarship, especially if they are an athlete, but there are thousands of scholarships that students do not apply for.

Make sure you look at my bonus chapter for more ideas on where to find scholarships.

Unable to Visit

As January 2021 approached, we found ourselves in a cyclone of interviews. We were consumed by the virtual campus visits. The schools were trying to figure out how to get prospective students and their families on their campus safely. Many of them fell short, and understandably so. But others thought outside the box, and their creativity and innovation came into play. One school had an interesting way to conduct tours via YouTube. They recorded students on different parts of the campus, explaining the history or the intricacies of where they were. Another school gave out maps and a recording, so you could listen to the tour as you drove around the school on your own.

We spent countless hours on Zoom calls and webinars; it was unbelievable. We visited some schools two or three times via Zoom because we liked what they said but we needed more information. We were trying to get a feel for the campus. But when you're on Zoom, you don't get the essence of the school, nor do you get the smell of the campus. You can't feel the energy, and you know I'm passionate about the energy around me.

Every school is different, and we just wanted to make the right decision, but he restriction from the pandemic made it difficult. There were several schools wanted to fly him out to see their campus. But if he caught COVID-19 while on the campus, he could not fly back. What a conundrum. I was not going to take that chance. I started to dive deeper into the tuition, and these schools were really expensive—how was I going to afford any of these schools with just a $500 scholarship? How was I going to make this work?

As we continued made our way through the interviews, there was one coach that really stood out. He personally took a group of perspective students on a tour through his campus, on his Discord channel. This was an unconventional tour, but it worked for the most part. The coach navigated through the school, showing them the highlights and, of course, the lab. This was a good Idea, but they lost connection a few times. Bottom line my son got to see the campus. No matter how unconventional it was. Everyone was trying to help us feel like we were a part of their family.

This was more difficult than you could imagine. In 2019, when my older son stepped out of the car and onto the campus he had just graduated from, he said this was where he belonged, and I wanted that same feeling for my younger son. It did not look like it was going to happen.

Chapter 6

What Are We Doing?

How Do I Help My Son Find a School?

I was getting wrapped up in finding an Esports Varsity team and not a school with his major. I was lost. It is important to make sure, he loved the school and remember college is for learning, but Esports can help you pay for it. That is a quote I came up with much later, but it works.

As we continued our quest to find a collegiate Esports Varsity team, the amount of e-mail was exasperating. How could someone continuously send out so many e-mails over and over again? I understand that the schools were looking for players because there weren't enough players to go around, but the more e-mails I got, the more I sent them to spam. Back then, colleges needed to promote their program more, and not constantly send the same e-mails to the same people. We clearly had to stop all of these emails. We had to get it down to ten schools in a hurry. Ten schools would be more manageable. This secretary had a full-time job, and when I got off work, I had to go through the e-mails. I was tired.

If I knew then what I know now, he would have only applied to the top ten Esports collegiate programs that kept popping up in my Google search, and that would have been that. I didn't see the full picture. I didn't know. How could I?

When it came time for my son to tell the schools he would not be attending in the fall, I told him he needed to send them an e- mail or contact them on discord. It is the right thing to do.

The time had come, and he finally got the list down to ten schools. The first schools to get removed from the list were the ones that kept the tournament winnings. The second schools to get taken off the list were the ones that said he had to commit to the school before he tried out for the team, and then it was the schools that said everybody plays.

With that being said - It was time for my son to do a very difficult task of notifying the schools he was not going to attend. You never know when you will have to cross that bridge again. One coach said that nobody had ever send him an email like that before, and he admired him for doing it. I was happy my son did not go to that school because the coach left about 1 ½ years later. There was one school—you know, the one that said everybody plays— they were very disrespectful. They told my son to call up admissions and withdraw his application. I could tell they were upset but they could have handled it better. I was so happy he removed that school from the list.

As he removed schools from the list, he removed their banner from the wall. Narrowing down schools to one, was becoming difficult.

We Got a College Visit In

As spring 2021 rolled in, campuses started to give tours. The campus scene was bustling once again. We were trying to figure out which school or schools we were going to visit. We had to see at least one or two. I didn't want to be in big crowds, but if this was going to help my son choose a school, I was going to "suck it up." We decided to go to three campuses. Why we chose those schools, I do not know. They made sense at the time.

We arrived at the first school, and they still had a lot of COVID-19 restrictions in place. I was OK with that. We checked in and they gave us some merch. We walked around the campus, which took 5 mins, literally. It was a really small campus. We sat in on the informational session and then we walked over to the lab, but it was not completed. This is not good, I thought to myself. The coach showed us the design, but was it going to be ready on time? Was this school for him? I didn't like it. There was a gloomy feeling on this campus and in the classroom. The paint on the walls were so dark, it didn't make me want to go to class. It was not inviting. How can anyone learn in a dungeon? Did I say that? This is why it is important to walk on a college campus. A week later, we were off to visit another school.

We arrived on the campus, and it was smaller than I thought but a lot bigger than the last college we had visited, and a lot cleaner. The campus was quiet; barely anyone was walking around. But I could see how busy the school could be. We went to the athletic compound to meet the coach. When we walked into the state-of-the-art building, where the coach and two Esports players were waiting for us, I was delighted with all the pictures, welcoming monuments, bright walls and high ceilings. This building was immaculate.

The only thing I didn't like was the person sitting at the desk. He did not ask us for any identification. Was it because we were with the coach? That shouldn't matter. Security is important to me.

They escorted us around the building so that we could get a better feel for the school's atmosphere. Then it happened we walked into the lab. I was mesmerized. This was the first lab I had seen up close. It took me back to OGF 2018. There was not one console to be found: nothing but gaming PCs. I was excited because, as you read, not every school's lab was ready; they were still in the process of building them.

Moments later some of the players came into the lab and started to get ready for a competition. They were focused and did not care that we were standing there. Since I did not know the protocol, I was not going to say anything and interrupt their flow. We left our son in the lab and walked over to another area where the coach wanted to talk to us about the program and the school. A conversation with a coach or director is extremely important.

The Coach they pulled out his golf cart and took us for a private tour of the school. We even got to see the living arraignments of one of the players.

When we got to the third and final school, we were able to walk around the entire campus with a tour guide. Covid restrictions were starting to ease up. I was not impressed; in fact, I was extremely bored, so I know my son was beyond bored. But since he had practiced with this team before, we felt obligated to take an official tour. I would have loved to see the lab, but they did not let us see it. They did make us feel like family, but I didn't feel any energy here, and I guess that's why I shut down early; but in the end, it was still his decision.

Creating Lasting Friendships

With the exception of one coach, every other coach and director was supportive and forthcoming. That's pretty good odds—one out of Twenty-five coaches and directors. They were dedicated to their Esports program, and that was one of the reasons it was going to be a difficult decision. So much pressure.

The conversations with the coaches became more intense and more frequent, not in a bad way. Just me nitpicking and trying to find out more about their school. That is when I discovered that most of the Esports scholarships were more than $500 a year. I could not believe the amount of money schools were offering for Esports. This was going to be interesting. My son was also offered an honors scholarship from every school, and I was happy until they told me that it would not cover dormitory expenses. If the scholarship was from the school and it went over the cost of tuition, he could not use it. Bottom line, school-based scholarships could not exceed the cost of the tuition in some of the schools. But yet, they wanted him in the honors program. Now, if he agreed to go to a school that was out of state, we would have more of a financial responsibility. How could we decide on what school to attend when Mommy's ATM was on strike? Why would we pay more money? There were so many factors that had to go into deciding on a school he loved.

We started to get closer to the deadline. I know I was driving all of the coaches crazy with my relentless questioning. I needed more information. This was all new to me. Thank God the coaches understood what I wanted. They were really patient with me. I know they told me the truth about their schools. It was all up to my son.

But there was one director that really saw my struggle, and he told me that he would not take it personally if we did not choose his program. As a matter of fact, he told me that he would help us figure out the right school for my son. What more could a gaming mother ask for? I was starting to feel the love from the Esports community.

My consistent questioning helped me to build a strong bond with several coaches, and over the years, I have watched the coaches' become directors, move on to different schools, and achieve greatness. We still talk and text each other about the world of Esports and the direction Esports is going. They had been a preiceless resource to me, throughout the recruitment process and still today.

Colleges Were Too Far

We had ten schools left on the list. They were all at least a 4-hour drive or a 2-hour plane ride away. Why hadn't the East Coast embraced the world of Esports? This was frustrating. We need more choices. We only found a few. There was still one school on the East Coast and one school upstate that was still on the list, but the scholarship money was lower than any other school. The schools on the East Coast did not offer a scholarship because they had just started their Esports program. They had not proven to the administration that Esports was a viable, sustainable program.

I walked into the gaming room that was still there, and I sat in the gaming chair and laid back, looking up at the schools' banners that were still taped on the wall. "Will I be able to get out of this chair?" I thought. That was when my puppy took the opportunity to lay her head on my leg and give me some comfort. Praying for guidance and direction, I wanted the school to jump off the wall and say, "Pick me!" But everything remained still; nothing moved. I was hoping for something to magically fall off the wall.

I continued to look at the names, but nothing happened. I heard my son walked into the kitchen, and I asked him to join me. I asked him if he had given any thought about which school he wanted to attend. I said: "This is your future and whatever happens is your decision. I am here to help guide you, but you make the final choice. Look at them. Are any of them calling your name?"

Both of us sat there in silence. I told my son to get the interview sheets, so we could review them again. Now that the list was shorter, we could pinpoint certain details that the coaches had said. "What coach made you feel comfortable? What coach seems to be interested in you as a whole person? What coach will take care of you when you're away from me?"

My son said, "Ma, I know what school I like, but you're going to tell me it's too far away." Well, he was not wrong about that. So, I told him to take his time, but he had a week to decide what school he wanted to attend.

With all the roads leading out of state, I had to sit back and wait. I hoped we would get enough scholarship money to cover most of the cost. He was awarded scholarships from outside organizations, but was it going to be enough?

Breaking It Down

Coaches were starting to get on edge and were wondering when my son and the other players were going to commit. He had to make a decision. My son had chosen his final five schools. The removal of five banners from the wall was complete. I wanted to play a sad song, but I didn't. There were two schools I had wished he hadn't taken off the wall, but it was his decision.

The official commitment day was May 1st, but I wanted him to get this over with, so I told him I wanted to know by April 25th. So, I created 5 beautiful drinking glasses; each one displayed the school's name in the school's colors. They were strategically placed on the entertainment center in the living room. Every time someone went pass them, they we reminded of the big decision that had to be made.

He started breaking down the pros and the cons once again. All the schools had his major and a Varsity Esports program. Each school was farther than the other; not one was in our state.

But there was one coach that always stood out more than the others. He stood out because he was following everything my son was doing. He would comment on his wins—and his losses, which were few. He would coach him on the things he did right and wrong in the game. Then the biggest surprise came when he told my son the scholarship, they were offering. I said that has to be for four years. My son said, "No, Ma, that's for one year." We went back and forth for a couple of minutes, and I said, "Call the coach. I need to hear it from him." When I got on the phone, the coach was laughing, and he said, "I want your son to play on my team, and that amount is for one year, not four."

After talking to the coach, I found out that one of my son's contenders' teammates played on his Varsity Esports. So, had my son made his decision already? Was he stringing me along the entire time because he knew deep down inside that he wanted to play with his friend? I'll never know what really happened. All I knew was that there was one week to go and there were still five glasses on the entertainment center.

When it came to our financial responsibility to pay the schools, there really wasn't that much of a difference. So, he could have gone anywhere at this point.

One by one, a glass would disappear off the shelf, and then there was one! He signed a letter of intent, and it was done. This level was complete.

Chapter 7

Becoming an Empty Nester

Preparing to Send Both of My Sons Off to College

Time was flying by, and it was almost time to send both of my young men off to college. I patiently waited to see when the first day of school was going to be for both of them, and thankfully, they were a week apart. I could not believe they were going to be away from home. They had been to summer camp before and the house was empty, but this was different. They were going to experience new things with new people—maybe even a broken heart or be a heart breaker. Endless opportunities were waiting for them.

My living room was a mess; it was like a cyclone had hit it. For some reason, no one could put their college stuff in their bedrooms. I had to buy two of everything; sometimes three or four—the never-ending saga of Mommy's ATM. The bins were getting full, and they were starting to pile up high on top of each other. Every bin had a list taped to the side of it, to make sure there were no doubles—a little OCD.

My oldest son made this moving extravaganza more intense by not coordinating with his roommates in what I considered a timely manner. I just needed to know who was bringing what for the apartment. It was like pulling teeth. The off-campus apartment had a full-size bed, so we could not use the extra-long twin sheets anymore. Mommy's ATM was open for business again, and it was quickly starting to evaporate. He needed a new laptop, and things for the kitchen and his personal bathroom. I could go on and on, but you get the picture.

It gets better—or does it? Apparently, my younger son was also moving into an off-campus apartment. This university only had off-campus apartments. Open up that wallet, lady, and get that card out. How much was the scholarship again?

Throughout this entire process, I was numb as I watched my bank account dissolve right before my eyes. There is always something new to buy, especially when you have an Esports player that is playing on a PC. It seemed like his equipment would become obsolete the day after I bought it.

We had to make sure that the PC was up to date for casual play. Who was I kidding at this point? There was no such thing as casual play. I had a hardcore gamer. He was an Esports player. I am not pretending that I knew what that meant; I still had a lot to learn.

Driving to the School Esports University

We were all packed up and ready to drive ten hours to my son's new adventure. I didn't buy everything he needed because we needed room in the car for the family. So, I was going to wait to buy the household items when I got to the school. The only thing he was worried about was his PC, of course. I meticulously fit everything into the car with not one inch to spare. Everyone was comfortable and we were on our way.

I was starting to feel a little melancholy and I was second guessing his decision to go to a school that was almost 550 miles away. Why did he really pick this school? Was it because the coach was so attentive in helping him? Was it because one of the players on the team played with him in contenders? Whatever the reason, we were on our way and there was no turning back now.

Whenever we went on a long trip, my children always wondered how I knew the words to so many songs. It was easy; I listened to music all the time, growing up, especially on Saturdays when the family cleaned the house. Music and laughter always filled my childhood home.

We were finally out of city traffic and on the open road, so I settled into my seat for the long drive, and I drove for almost 6 hours. It was time to stretch our legs and get some gas. I did all the hard work by driving through Pennsylvania. I couldn't believe how huge that state is. We finally arrived at the school, and the first thing I said was, "I will never do that again. We will only fly and ship everything—and I mean everything."

We were getting my son settled in, and what do you think his main concern was? Where he should put his PC. We had to find the ethernet outlet; it was on the other side of the apartment, near the front door. This meant a trip to the store. We found a Best Buy one town over. When we got back to the apartment we helped him with the groceries

And finish setting up his PC. He was ready for us to leave just like most college students. But like a mom, I had to talk to his roommates. I wanted to see where they were from, what they were up to, and what their plans were. And just like typical college students, they told me what they thought I wanted to hear. I saw right through the nonsense.

I was not ready to leave him yet, so all of us got back in the car, and we drove around the town, checking out the area. It was a quaint little town. If you blink your eyes and you would miss it. We found a BBQ place to have dinner. After dinner, we headed to the grocery store to fill up his refrigerator. We drove back to campus and dropped him off and headed to the hotel to get some rest for the long journey that awaited us in the morning.

I know you want to know what school he chose. That is just one of the mysteries in the world of Esports. That is his story to tell.

Returning Home Without My Esports Player

This was going to be a difficult day. We were going to leave our baby boy at college. He would be 550 miles away from home. I was leaving my son in the hands of a coach, someone that had committed to help develop his growth while he engaged in different challenges in his new chapter. Was I asking too much, or was I not asking enough? I checked and double checked to make sure he didn't need anything else before we left. I didn't want to leave knowing I forgot something.

Well, it was time to leave. I did not want to. Hey! I remembered seeing a help wanted sign for the school. They were looking for security officers. I could quit my job and stay there. Wait! My job was remote; I did not have to quit. I could do my remote job during the day and work security at night. I know! Stop it! I was being overprotective. Let him go and grow, Mother!

I reluctantly got behind the wheel of the car and we were on our way home. As we reached the Pennsylvania turnpike, tears started to fall from my eyes. I wasn't going to see him until Thanksgiving, and this was going to be another challenge for me. We had never been apart that long. What if something happened? Did his roommates already have COVID-19? Did they practice precautions? Of course, not; they're college students. Just keep him in prayer. He will be fine.

Finally, we made it through the Pennsylvania turnpike, and it was smooth sailing—or was it? There was a lot of traffic. Does everyone have a car? This is ridiculous. When we got home, I walked into his room, which was kind hallow. The laughter that once came from this room when he was playing a game on his PC was gone. I sat in his gaming chair, thinking about how much I missed him. His PC was gone, and everything felt different.

I started to clean up his room and look for things he might have left. It looked like he did not forget anything, and he should be good. The next day, I went back into his room and cleaned everything up. I washed all the sheets and quilts. I prepared his room for his Thanksgiving visit. I guess we could Facetime until then.

I took a picture, sent it to him and said, "You are welcome."

There was still one young man to go, so snap out of it and let's get him ready for his new adventure.

Driving the Oldest Child to School Still Had a Lot of Restrictions

While still trying to come to grips with the fact that my gamer was so far away, it was time to take my older son to school. This was not going to be as overwhelming. This was our third year taking him to college, and we did not have to drive 20 hours.

He has his own car, and I could not stop laughing when I saw it was overflowing with stuff he wanted to take to college. There was no way he was going to get all of that stuff in his car and drive safely. He had too much. We had already planned to drive two cars up to the school anyway, but I didn't know how much he was going to take. Now I needed to organize both cars. Unbelievable!

There were two good things about this trip: It was a turnaround trip, meaning we didn't have to stay overnight; we could drive up to the school, get him settled, and drive right back. Also, the entire trip took less time. About 6 ½ hours. In some strange way, this felt like we were taking him to college for the first time.

This was big; we were not dropping him off at the dorm. He was going to live with three other young men in an off-campus apartment. This would bring a whole new world of responsibility. Adulting would be different.

We started on our way; my husband rode with him, for some last-minute male talk. I rode alone in my car, with the radio playing the music I wanted to hear. But since I was alone, I had to keep a keen eye out for the deer. They could come from anywhere. They had surprised me in the past. I knew the way, but I listened to the GPS this time. I had to watch for deer.

I got to the apartment complex 2 minutes before they did—and they had been driving in front of me the whole time. We all arrived safely, with no deer sightings.

We started to unpack the cars, and there was a staircase that we had to walk up to get to the apartment. He was on the first floor—why were there stairs? After my first trip up the stairs, I said, "Hey, guys, I'll catch up with you in a minute. I'm going to the bathroom." I took this time to snoop around the apartment and see what was going on. After all, I was paying for it. By the way, I was asked to transport the stuff to the school not the apartment. No one said anything about putting it in the apartment. So, I let my son and his father do all the work.

This apartment was really nice. There were four bedrooms and all of them had a private bathroom. The living room was a nice size, and the kitchen was beautiful with state-of-the-art appliances. The washer and dryer were nestled in a closet with folding doors to hide behind. As I walked across the living room and looked out the window, I noticed a BBQ pit. I wondered how much use they would get out of it because it gets really cold, really quick up here. Everything was in the apartment except his friends. They would be up later in the day.

It was getting late, and I wanted to eat before we hit the road, so all of us went out to lunch. Of course, there were things he had to get, because I told him what he needed and he told me he didn't—hmm, teenagers. Was I this difficult? Nah!!

As much as he wanted us to leave, we wanted to get out of that mountain area and back to sea level. We jumped in the car and made our way back home while looking for deer along the way.

Filled with emotions, I could not believe I was going home to an empty house.

Returning to an Empty House

Walking into the house for the very first time, knowing that both of my young men were not at home, was awkward. Who was going to try my patience today? Who was going to try to go places they shouldn't be going? Who was going to try to stay on their PC all night? Now that they were in college, was that something they were going to do? What was going to happen to their grades? I prayed that the educational aspect of college was going to take precedence.

I felt alone but I was beaming with pride. I did all I could to keep them on the right path and I did a great job. My older son had been able to maintain a 4.0 GPA in college for two years, and now we would see if my younger son was going to do the same.

I walked into my oldest son's room, as I always did after he went to college, and cleaned it. I washed everything, put everything back neatly, took a picture of it, and sent it to him and said, "You are welcome!"

Well, at least I still had work to keep me a little busy. But how long would that be? I could still get a job at my younger son's school. LOL.

I created a spreadsheet with both of my young men's schedules on it, color-coded to the school they were attending. This way, I would know when I could text or call them. I hung it in the hallway near the kitchen; with easy access for me and my husband to see.

This only made me miss them more. With each passing moment I felt the emptiness in my heart. Funny how the stillness of the house could make you miss someone more.

I held out as long as I could. It had been 6 weeks, and the gamer did not want to face time with me. What didn't he want me to see. So, I had to take matters into my own hands. Why not visit my gamer in school? I was about to have a three-day weekend. I knew he was coming back the next month, but I still needed to see him; I wanted to make sure he was OK. I booked a seat on Delta and flew out to Detroit. The plane landed earlier than it was scheduled, and I could only hope that the rental car was ready, and it was. Let's just hope the Hotel room is ready. It was and I checked into the hotel. Everything was flowing. I felt Like I should be here. After I settled in, I texted my son. "I will see you in about an hour." He texted back, "No, you won't." This was the first time he text me back so fast. Then, moments later, he texted again and said, "Oh, you're here?" I could only imagine the look on his face when he saw I was only an hour away. What was he thinking as life 360 pinpointed my location? He was adulting and mommy was coming to see him. How dare I mess up his flow.

I started on my way to the school, and I got there really fast. The speed limit is 75 MPH. Just insane! I may or may not drive that fast on occasion, but its only me and not everyone on the highway. I arrived at the school and parked the car in front of his apartment. I texted him to come downstairs. When I saw him walk out of the apartment complex, I was relieved, he looked really good. We hugged, we laughed, and we joked for hours like we always did; I needed that!

It was time for him to go to practice. I gave him a big hug and told him how much I loved him, and he reciprocated. He missed me. I watched him walk into the apartment complex and then I drove away. I still didn't know if this was the right school. On my way back to the hotel, while driving that insane speed with everyone else, I got a flat tire. I couldn't believe this was happening. I pulled over to the side of the road as fast as I could. I was scared to get out of the car. The cars and trucks were flying by so fast that my car shook with every passing vehicle. I called the service affiliated with the rental car, and they said, "Can you try to get off that highway? We do not service cars on that highway." WHAT? In my Whoopie Goldberg voice from *Ghost*, I said, "You in danger girl." Maybe they should lower the speed limit. I looked to see how far the exit was, and I said: "I am staying right here." What was I going to do? I could not stay here all night.

What a minute I have AAA. I called them and they asked for my coordinates and said: "we will be right there." Thank God someone was brave enough to help me. I looked to see how close I was to the exit again and I said to myself: "you can make it." I drove the car onto the grass, and I started to move slowly towards the exit. Finally, I was off that deadly highway. I called AAA back and told them I was off the exit; within two minutes, the tow truck arrived. They fixed the tire, and I was back on that insane highway. Would I do it all over again? Of course, I would. It was all worth it.

Too Much Time on My Hands

With each passing day, I found out that I had a little more time than the day before. I had too much time on my hands, and I didn't know what I was going to do. I was still working, but the time I enjoyed with my children had come to an abrupt halt. I had to fill that void.

We still had some COVID-19 restrictions, so there wasn't much I was comfortable doing. I started to walk around my neighborhood. First, I walked halfway to the elementary school and back. That was about 1-mile round trip. For about a week, I did one mile, and that became easy, and it was extremely boring because nobody else was outside. I decided to challenge myself and walk a 5K, which is 3.1 miles. I didn't want to walk around my neighborhood anymore, so I decided to drive to the local park.

Let's just say a 5K was a little more than I thought it was going to be, so the first time out, I only did 2 miles. But there was an energy in the park that I didn't have when I walked around my neighborhood; there were people. They would say "good morning" and "how are you?" as they walked by me. This helped me to get through the walk. And within two weeks, I had finally completed a 5K. I was so excited. I had fulfilled my goal and conquered the beast.

The 5k took me about 55 mins, and I had to get the time down. With a lot of determination, I was able to cut off 15 minutes within a month, and another 5 minutes the next month. I was feeling like a pro, and I had started to fill the void I had in my heart when my young men went to college. This was no substitute for them, but it gave me a sense of accomplishment and self-worth. I started to enter 5k races/walks. No, I did not win but I did okay.

One day My supervisor asked me to join a special team that would help more people that had contracted COVID-19. This new position allowed me to schedule more hours on certain days, while allowing me to have more days off. I hesitated at first, but she convinced me that I would be helping more people. So, I agreed.

While walking in the park on my day off, I started to think about Esports. I didn't know why but it was heavy on my mind. Where was this coming from and what was I going to do about it? Nothing, I thought to myself. But when I got home from my walk, I started to google Esports. What was compelling me to do this? My son was in college, and I had completed the journey. The rest was up to him. He was on a Varsity Esports team and there was nothing else for me to do. I was finished.

It had been a few months since I thought about Esports and for some reason I was being pulled back in. What was going on? I followed the direction I was being told to go and I found a whole new world. Where did this come from? I was trying to fight this, but it was clear that this was the path I was supposed to follow. I found myself unraveling more and more every day. I could not stop.

Chapter 8

The Transformation

Setting Goals

As you know, I've always had a schedule for the schedule, and everything has always been extremely meticulous and sometimes overwhelming. Work was the only thing that consumed my time. Funny how work gets in the way of fun. Our days and hours would change all the time. One week, we worked for 30 hours; one week, we worked for 24 hours, and then it was back to 30 hours. I am not complaining; I had nothing else to do.

In the midst of all this free time, I decided to start setting some goals. I took early morning walks to clear my head and prepare for the next 5k. I prayed for my family and those near and dear to me. I asked for guidance, and I was pointed back in the direction of Esports. Why? My sons were in college, doing their thing and creating their new chapter. I didn't think there was a reason for me to continue anything in the world of Esports ever again. It was over; I was done. Well, I was wrong. I struggled with this day after day but I was given the vision to help parents understand the world of Esports. Why should they try to figure this out on their own, when I had the answers?

I started out with four simple goals:

- Help families find a collegiate Esports Varsity team or programs for their child(ren).
- Made a list of all the schools that had Esports programs in the United States.
- Talk to more coaches.
- Understand the Esports program at the college level.

These goals seemed realistic and attainable. Well, the reality of trying to obtain this information became abundantly clear. Besides the coaches I had spoken to during the recruitment process, I had no one else that I could talk to. The other coaches were very hard to reach; there was nothing on their website that could direct me to them. There were coaches that were hesitant to speak with me. I did not understand why they did not want to talk to me. I was trying to help families understand Esports as a legitimate program.

I was determined to get answers, and I was not going to let these hiccups stand in the way of me achieving the ultimate challenge of understanding Esports. The Esports community was blossoming, and there were thousands of hands trying to mold the perfect vase. Everyone's intentions were admirable, and information started to pour in like a broken dam.

I was like a sponge, and I sucked it all up. I started documenting everything. I had a notebook for everything:

- One-on-one conversations
- Conferences
- Podcasts

- Classes I attended
- Upcoming events

I still have all the books. Are they outdated now? Of course, they are, but it is the history of my transition and it keeps me grounded.

Researching

As I researched, I found a lot of programs that explained the ideologies behind Esports, but which one should I believe? Who could I trust? There were two things everyone had in common: 1. To educate and elevate everyone's knowledge about the world of esports. 2. Esports are video games that are played at a highly organized competitive level, that have been around for years.

As I sorted through the information, I found one source that became my saving grace. It was a nonprofit Esports foundation that promoted the educational aspect of Esports, and they donated PCs to schools. Let me tell you, it took me no time to consume this information, I was so hungry, I could not wait to get to the next chapter. The deeper I got, the more I wanted. I was able to navigate the wonders of the evolving world of Esports on a daily basis. I have always been a great speaker but thanks to this foundation, I was able to talk to people confidently about Esports.

The need to quench my thirst continued; I found more programs that were going to help me lay the foundation for parents, guardians, grandparents, mentors, and school administrators. I was becoming the bridge that was going to bring the generations together. I was a machine, an AI in progress.

There were new opportunities everyday but for about a week, every time I got on my computer, there was one organization that kept popping up. It kept saying they were pioneers in the world of Esports and they were doing great things in Atlanta. No matter where I turned or what I did, the name continued to pop up. I searched for more info, and I found out that they were teaching coding to high school students. I was intrigued. I wanted to see this for myself, so I contacted them, and they said I could come through. The next thing I knew, I was on a Delta flight to Atlanta, GA to see their magic.

When I got there, I was amazed to see the camaraderie between the instructors and the students. The respect resonated throughout the room as young minds were captivated by the learning process. The instructors were superior to anyone I had ever seen before. They found a way to educate teens. The instructors were able to pull the students into their world and teach them something new and exciting. They were able to keep students excited about learning and they were curious to learn more. Little did the students know, this was going to transform their lives and reshape their future.

Before I knew it, it was time for me to head back home. I wanted to stay longer but I was worried about the Atlanta traffic and the huge airport. I would probably have to run through the airport to make my flight on time. If I had known that I would have been intoxicated by this program, I would have booked a later flight.

When I got home, I dove deeper into the world of Esports. I found classes that would explain why Esports was needed. I learned how to start an Esports club in both the middle schools and high schools, and I even got certified as an Esports club sponsor. Can you believe that this lady was on her way to becoming an expert in Esports?

I started to soar like a phoenix.

Full Immersion

My eyes were completely open now, and I had finally caught the bug that my young men had for years. The amount of information I was absorbing allowed me to be a part of a new world that was transcending my thoughts and letting me explain Esports to everyone I met: World of Esports 101. I was able to talk to parents that did not like the gaming world because they do not understand it. I was able to talk to parents from my personal experience and not just from what I had read. I was talking to anyone that would listen; no matter where we went, I would talk about Esports. I even talked about it at church events. I couldn't contain the passion I had for Esports—I was becoming an intricate member of this world.

There was no going back at this point, and I didn't want to stop. I was consumed by the carrot that was dangling before me. I was looking for some pictures on my phone, when I came across several pictures, I had taken at the Overwatch Grand Finals in 2018 and laughed. Look at me now 2018 Karen! We did it! It was inevitable.

Colleges all over the world started implementing Esports programs and I had to focus, dig deep and search for more colleges and Universities that have an Esports program. I started a spreadsheet with easy indicators: school name; state; Esports Varsity team, club, or business degree program. Of course, I started with the 10 schools that kept showing up on Google, and the next thing I knew, I was up to 200 schools. Now I have over 680 schools that have an Esports program. It is not easy to get on my list you have to have a sustainable

Esports program that respect their players and have the support of the administration. I am very particular about the schools that make my list. While my team and I were searching Esports Programs, we found a growing amount of HBCU's (Historically Black Colleges and Universities) that have an Esports program. Esports is everywhere.

I have to give credit where credit is due. Every school that I put on the list, my team works hard to make sure they have a program that is up and running. We check them once and sometimes twice a year. Right now, they are updating schools that added new title to their list.

I started telling my friends about all the wonderful things I was learning, and they became interested in Esports. Not long after that, I was talking to administrators and I was able to Bridge the Gap. Hey! I like that name: "Bridging the Gap in Esports."

As time went on, I started to meet more people in the industry, and this was a blessing in disguise. They were happy to know that someone was talking to parents on a local level.

Attending Conferences and Listening to Podcasts

This industry is rapidly growing and there are endless opportunities for me to explore. The people I met in the industry directed me towards conferences and podcasts. There was something to listen to almost every day. This was going to enhance everything I was learning and hopefully bring it all together. Most, if not all, conferences were still online, and this was a good way for me to study the industry. I realized that Esports is bigger that I could Imagine.

The conferences were a portal into the uncharted world. I got to see the inner workings of high school and collegiate Esports. I only wish I knew this in 2020. "Water under the bridge," as my grandmother would say. "Just move forward and forge ahead." But now I understood all the challenges I had faced when trying to get my son into a college with Esports. The strategies were clear to me, and I knew how to maneuver through the process.

I dubbed myself the conference queen. I was juggling two or three conferences and sometimes four at the same time. I had nothing but time. I started to spread my wings and reach out to more people, and they would tell me where to find more conferences. About three or four months into attending online conferences, I could not believe I still had so much more to learn.

My favorite conferences and podcasts were the ones that coaches were featured on. I loved their view on Esports, and I wanted to know what they were going to do and how they were going to grow their programs. I listened attentively because this allowed me to be able to develop questions to ask them about their programs.

I had so many revelations. I should have gone right, instead of going left so many times, in the past.

Discovering the Magic of Esports

As a Disney girl, I am always looking for the magic in everything, and as I continued to get deeper into the world of Esports, I started to see the magic. I started to pull away the layers of the onion and saw that the magic went way past gaming.

For years, I called it a phase or just another trend that would come to an end. I really believed it was a Phase. But now, it was becoming my way of life, and I was enjoying my journey into the portal every day. In life you are either running in a race or enjoying the journey. I was enjoying the journey. As one great coach said: "Fulfill your purpose." And I was doing that.

Once I understood the magic, I saw that it was everywhere. My pilgrimage through Esports became one of self-discovery, and self-growth. I started to learn how to do it, I saw how far I could drive myself and how easily I got manipulated in the beginning by falling into the pathway of the gaming universe. What was once foreign was now second nature to me. I was no longer intimidated. The opportunities were endless. What's scarier than a mom that really understands Esports? Recently I was talking to a coach and asked: "Where is your program housed?" He was shocked. He said: "you know what you are talking about." Most people do not know to ask that question.

Feeling confident about my Esports knowledge, I cut down the amount of time I was in conferences and listening to podcasts. I worked on developing my program and building it up. It was not always a bed of roses, but it is magical when I stood in front of a group of parents, grandparents, mentors, and students. It was hard to contain my passion for Esports.

What I loved most about Esports at this point was that I understood what gamers were talking about, and I could contribute to the conversation. That is really important to me.

Every day brought new ideas. I was bubbling over with creativity, and it had been a long time since my creative genius was able to enhance the world.

As I worked on everything that was coming my way, I felt like I was doing the tango, slowly and intricately putting everything into place. I was turning my head quickly towards a new idea, leaning back further to reach for something to add to the pot, so that it could stir up a magical experience for those who wanted to learn.

Chapter 9

Talking to the Community

Educating Parents, Grandparents, Guardians, Mentors, and Administrators

The time had come once again to really immerse myself in educating everyone about the world of Esports.

My meetings were very humble: just a few people, one-on-one calls, libraries, parent events, and gaming labs. It became a way of life to just talk about Esports. Before I knew it, I was being flown every where to help parents understand Esports. This was amazing.

All of a sudden, people were reaching out to me globally. Everyone wanted to learn about Esports and what I thought about it. They wanted to know what this humble little mom felt about the ever-changing world of Esports. Me! This was life changing. I have to tell you that all of this was great, but it would be the look on a teenager's face when I started to talk about video games in their language, that filled my heart with joy. They could not believe a mom understood the gaming world.

Every time I finished a presentation, the students come up to me and say, "How do you know all that? You're a mom." Yes, I am a mom, but how different is this from learning about baseball, football, soccer, or lacrosse? The students agreed.

Everything worthwhile takes time and I am still a work in progress. As my calendar continues to fill up, I thank God for my friends that supported me and continue to do so today. They talk to their friends about what I am doing as much as I talk about it. I have transformed their lives.

Recently, I went to a neighborhood event Just to hang out and ran into the organizers of the event. They told me that they were having a hard time getting people to come to their meetings. I allowed them to finish telling me about all the different things they were doing, and then I said, "Hey, how about having a game night? The children can play while I talk to the parents about the world of Esports? She said, "What a great idea!" The event was a success. The audience was extremely interactive and now they want to have tournaments.

I have had a lot of great times in the World of Esports, but there have also been some valleys. Were their people I should not have collaborated with or given them the time of day? Yes! But it is all a part of the learning curve. I just got up and reinvented my programs. I got out of situations that did not follow my values, and those experiences are for another book.

Competition

A lot of the parents and educators want to know about competitions and where they are. When it comes to competition, there are several levels.

Competitions are everywhere for everyone. They are online or a LAN (Local Area Network). In my neighborhood, LAN completions are becoming popular, finally. There are different gaming communities (game titles) that meet each week and display their skills in friendly competition. There are popular completion's all around the world like Dreamhack, Red Bull, EVO and Championship playoff for the Major titles like: Dota 2, League of Legends, Overwatch, Rocket League, and a host of others.

For several years, I was trying to figure out the competitive side and how it works. I am still a work in process. The competitions are intense. If it is online, I check back every few minutes to see the score. If is in person, I feed off the energy and watch the game. During the pandemic era, Esports was the only competitive sport that had competitions and the fan base was able to watch.

When we got into the collegiate scene, I noticed that many of the players that were in contenders were also in the collegiate realm. Most of the players were playing collegiate and contenders at the same time; and yes, most of them were definitely maintaining their GPA. The culture does not only compete on the Esports level; they brag about the teams GPA.

I watched as some of the collegiate players were being pulled into the league. I have no idea how this happened, but I found myself cheering for everyone who became a professional player. I wish I could make a fantasy Esports team. My team would win every week.

As far as the amateur league goes, you can find them almost anywhere, depending on your skill level and who you follow on Discord and Twitch. I have seen competitions that are free, some that cost $5, and many that have a high entry fee.

Let's talk about the league. I know it may be difficult for some of you to think about having a favorite professional Esports team, so let me ask you this. Who is your favorite professional football, baseball, or basketball team? As for me, I love who I love: Steelers, Yankees, Knicks and Cowboys. I know, I cannot love the Steelers and the Cowboys. But I do. So, why not have a favorite Esports Teams. Once you understand how it works – you will love it.

When it comes to the Collegiate level, I like the teams because of how they execute their programs. I do not care about their stats. The list below is because I have seen them grow. Nothing more and nothing less. So, here we go— my top ten favorite collegiate Esports programs in North America 2023:

- Northwood University
- Maryville University
- Illinois State University
- Boise State University
- Full Sail University
- Siena Heights University
- Winthrop University
- University of Akron
- University of Maryland
- SUNY Canton

Here are my favorite HBCU Teams 2023:

- Morgan State University
- Morris Brown University
- Morehouse College

Here are my all-time favorite Overwatch Contenders teams in North America that are still active in 2023. They are just fun to watch.

- Saints
- Wisp
- Redbirds
- Timeless

As far as the pro teams, I like London Spitfire because they were the team that won at OGF in 2018, but I also Like: Los Angeles Valiant, Washington Justice, and Dallas Fuel.

Explaining the Growth in Esports

Esports had grown a lot in a few years, and it was moving fast. I had to keep up, so I continued to grow with it. It is no longer ahead of me. The possibilities in Esports and how everyone can be a part of it is endless. Esports is not just for the young. It is for the young at heart and those willing to take the step to continue to have fun. Who says you have to stop having fun because you are a senior citizen? I have seen senior citizen Esports Leagues. They are amazing.

Esports allows people to grow with technology. The technology is unfolding faster every moment of every day. Look at all the conversations we are having about AI right now. Some people might find it hard to keep up with all the changes that are happening. That is why I created an in-person and virtual class for people to learn about the new technology and some of the legalities to watch out for.

When I look back into the history of Esports, I can remember putting a quarter on that game so I could play next, hoping that when I finally hit the high level, nobody would unplug it. Now I can sit in my living room and play on a console, or play on my phone with other people or play by myself.

Esports exploded so fast in 2020 that people thought it had just begun, but those of you who have been in the world of Esports since childhood, know it's been around since 1972, when Stanford had the very first competition and they called it an Olympic event. Since then, we have watched people win tournaments. They have gone from receiving Rolling Stones magazine subscriptions, a used Ferrari to millions of dollars.

There is no doubt in my mind or the minds of anybody else that 2020 set a precedence people played video games more than any other time. No need to go into all the specifics of 2020—most of us lived through it. Let's just say we had more time on our hands. Playing video games and talking with friends on Discord became a daily ritual. More parents became aware of video gaming, and so did educational institutions. Some embraced the journey some did not. This was a time for us to learn about video games; instead of shutting it out and pushing it away, we should have welcomed it. Today, in 2023 there are over 230 million people playing video games daily. We have come a long way.

One of the biggest attributes that grew Esports was the accessibility for spectators and fans to watch their favorite team or favorite player from almost anywhere. Thanks to online media outlets like Twitch and YouTube, fans were able to message people that were considered to be untouchable because they were famous. Collegiate, contender and pro players were interacting with their fans. The players showed the fans that they were just like them.

Who would have ever thought that you go to college and play video games and receive a scholarship for it, Unheard of! People are starting to see that esports is evolving and more people see the opportunities. How many college students do you know keep the winning from a tournament in a traditional sport? This is a very attractive incentive, and if you are lucky enough to know about it or even get on a team, you are ahead of the game.

Defining Esports

Plain and simple, Esports is not a phase. It is a way of life; it's a culture that overtook the digital world. They have their own language and values. It is a roller coaster ride of excitement. It is a thrilling ride; it is also a complex multifaced realm. And yes, there is more to Esports than collegiate, contenders, and pro leagues.

Esports has taken on one of the most controversial problems facing us today. They have taken on the mental health and well-being aspect of gaming, acknowledging how serious this is in our society today. Several organizations have been partnering with each other to help overcome the issue with mental health. There are classes online and workshops to help parents, caretakers, teachers, administrators, learn how to support a gamer that may have an addiction to video games. Mental health and staying healthy is serious, and I wanted to know how I could help. So, I became a certified mental health first aid responder. For me, it is important to be accessible and help anyone that may need Mental Health guidance. If you or someone you know needs help, please do not hesitate to call or text 988. Everything is confidential.

The Esports community is also embedded in recognizing how important it is to have inclusion and diversity. As I mentioned earlier in the book, girls have a hard time when they are playing video games, especially when they win. This is why it is important to have safe places for people to play. I have personally joined some of the clubs, and I found them to be quite refreshing. They create a healthy environment for everyone.

The business aspect of Esports has exploded. There are hundreds if not thousands of nonprofits and LLCs under the Esports umbrella, whose main goals are to empower those interested in any aspect in the world of Esports. This can be anything from being a coach, a director, an event organizer, an owner of a team and 100's more.

The technical innovation of Esports is changing every day, and it is phenomenal. The technology has proven to be groundbreaking, and it has opened up a new career paths.

Esports has shown us a new way to think and interact with one another.

Careers and Opportunities

Not too keen on playing video games? That's okay. There are hundreds of careers and opportunities in the world of Esports. Take Minecraft for example. It hep you learn about agriculture and engineering, and like every other game, it teaches you: collaboration, teamwork, real time strategies, and communication. Let me stop there for a minute because most people don't think video games educate children or young adults communication. You have to remember that their communication skills are different than when you grew up. I'm not talking about texting. When they are in a game, they talking to their teammates about what to do, how to do it, and how to bring it all together for the victory. Communication is an essential part of Esports, and we wouldn't have the champions we do if they didn't talk to each other.

Continuing with the skills that are learned in gaming:

- Problem solving
- Teamwork
- Patience
- Risk takers
- Perseverance
- Concentration
- Leadership
- Strategy
- Social skills
- Multitasking
- Critical thinking
- Pattern recognition
- Negotiation

- Self-control
- Networking
- Goal setting
- Creativity
- Analytical thinking
- Interpersonal skills
- Adaptability
- Focus
- And this next one is really dear to me because I work on this all the time: hand eye coordination. I actively keep up with my hand and eye coordination in the Metaverse when I play Beat Saber.

The skills you learn in gaming do not have to be used in an esports career:

One amazing transferable skill we found out was when my older son was a medical intern in college. He was learning how to work the robotic arm in the operating room and guess how you operate the robotic arm. With a gaming controller.

I am just going to list a few careers and opportunities that are in the world of Esports:

- Director
- Coach
- Broadcaster
- Content creator
- Manager
- Tournament organizer
- Data analyst
- Graphic designer

- Videographer
- Public relations
- Streamer/influencer
- Psychiatrist
- Operations manager
- IT
- Web developer
- Script Writer
- Event coordinator
- Live production technician
- Casting producer
- Analyst

Supporting Your Child

There are countless people who have been advised not to pursue their dreams. I was one of them. The worst advise I received from my family was to get a stable job; meaning to work for the government or have a traditional career path. Now, there is nothing wrong with those great professions. We always need someone to educate us and keep us safe. After all I followed a traditional path - law enforcement. But as the world continues to turn and technology is evolving. It is important to look towards new career path.

I never told my children what they should be when they grew up. They have always been free to choose their path. I allowed them to follow their dreams in gaming, and I didn't know I was going it. All I want is for my children is to be happy and have a fulfilling life. But you may need a back-up plan. I have spoken to my children on numerous occasions about having a back-up plan, just in case. This world is filled with

1000's of new and exciting opportunities. There is no reason for anyone to have a career they do not love. When I look back at my Job – I see that it was just that a Job. I learned the hard way that you should love what you do.

I supported my children in everything they did. I was always their biggest cheerleader. When they wanted to play Little League baseball, I had to learn the rules because it's not like regular baseball. Then it was flag football, and I had to learn the rules. Without naming every activity they were involved in, I had to learn the rules. Why was Esports so different? Was it because the face that people had put on gaming made it unappealing and unattractive for a parent to accept? Whatever it was and whatever it is, I missed out on a lot of good times because I didn't understand.

Supporting your child makes a world of difference; when they know you have their back, no matter what, it allows them to shoot for the stars.

Chapter 10

Purpose

Who Are You?

It was the end of the school year, and both of my young men were coming home from college. What was I going to do? I was so wrapped up in the world of Esports, How was I going to explain this to them? I wondered how they were going to react to all the information I had circulating in my head and flowing in my blood. Would they want to watch a game with me? Would they think it's crazy to watch a game with their mother?

They were not totally in the dark. They knew I was learning about Esports; they just didn't know how far I had gone. They would say I went too far. With each passing day, I grew more nervous than the day before. This was their niche. Were they going to understand why I did it or it was something I was enjoying? How long could I hide the way I felt.

My older son drove home, hugged me, took a shower, and went to bed. Well, that was easy. Hours later, he woke up, ate, and talked to me for hours about his friends and all of his adventures in college. I never got a chance to say anything about Esports.

A few days went by, and it was time for the ultimate test. My husband and I took a Delta flight to Detroit to pick up our gamer and we were going to drive back. I know I said I wouldn't do the drive again, but he had so much, we had to drive him home. We went to the car rental and picked up a minivan to drive back home. I was nervous all the way to his school. I don't know why; was it because I was having flashbacks of that insane highway or being unveiled as a real Esports mom. Long as I didn't say anything, he wouldn't know anything. We finally arrived, we packed up the car, he said goodbye to his friends, and we were on our way home.

How was I going to make it through 10 hours and not talk about Esports? It was all I talked about for months. My gamer nestled into his seat, put on his ear pods so he didn't have to hear whatever I had on the radio, and the next thing I knew, he was asleep. Well, this was going to be easy. I didn't have to say anything.

After a couple of hours of driving, we decided to stop to pick up something to eat. I wrestled him out of the seat so he could stretch his legs and pick out what he wanted. As we walked towards the building, I asked him about his team and how he thought they did, and all I got was, "Good."

"Could you give me a little bit more details than just good?"

He said, "Fine!"

"OK, so you've been in college for a year—do you know more than one word to say?"

"Yes, I do," he said as he laughed.

I was irritated. I saw where this was going, so I said, "In the game when your team became the champs, I really liked what you did! They were constantly on the attack, and you were relentlessly healing everybody and healing yourself at the same time. How were you able to do that and so quickly?" He took his ear pods out and gave me the look of, "What?" I said, "Yeah, you kept disturbing their attacks and there was chaos everywhere, and I guess at the end, you guys just gave your all. It was an epic battle."

He started to look around the parking lot as if he lost something and then turned me around and said, "Who are you?" We laughed and headed inside the building.

What Did You Do with Our Mother?

Working from home has its advantages and disadvantages. The best part about my job was flexibility; I had control of the hours I worked, and this allowed me to balance my lifestyle—or should I say my "Esports fix."

However, there are many challenges when you work from home. Just because my physical presence was in the house did not mean I was there for individual needs. Like what is for lunch? Did you make Dinner yet? So, I put a sign on top of my office door, and when the light was on, it meant I was working: Pretend that I am in a different physical building. That did not work. They would text me. All the time.

I quickly saw the hours I had scheduled were going to have to change to meet the needs of my family. Everyone was home. They slept late so I went to work early and then went on my walk in the afternoon. My entire schedule flipped. I wanted to watch the games, but I did not want them to know I was watching. What was I going to do? I cooked dinner and went in my office. As long as the food was cooked, they would not bother me. I locked the door and turned on the light, just in case. The only reason it worked was because the gamer was competing, and his brother was watching him from is bedroom.

I wanted my sons to accept and embrace the fact that we could talk about Esports, the games and the players because I knew everybody's name on the collegiate and contenders' level.

About a month after my young men had come home from school, we were making smores in the backyard. They started talking about Esports and I was busting inside. They started talking about certain players and I chimed in. They looked at me, looked at their father and went back to their conversation. As the night went on, I started to say more about games, tournaments, and players. I even started talking about a certain coach, and they said: "how do you even know that coach?" I know everyone. They laughed and said, "No, really, how do you know these people?" I go to events and I meet people that are passionate about esports. My older son said, "What did you do with our mother? This is crazy."

I said: "I improved the other model. In a world that needed a mother's point of view on the east coast, I became that mother."

My gamer said, "This is really weird. She's talking like she has known about Esports for years."

I walked inside to get more marshmallows and I overheard them say: "Why couldn't be like this year's ago?"

My True Purpose

In the back of my head, I always hear, "Stay true to your purpose"—simple little words that mean a lot. It has taken me through a journey that I didn't know I was destined to be on. I've always had a passion to educate, and it started with "Mommy Homework". My path was predestined, and until I dove deeper into it, I didn't know I was supposed to be an Esports Educator.

Sometimes you are put in situations that make you uncomfortable, like I was. I struggled to understand and support my children. I was in the deep end of the pool, trying to swim to the top. I learned to press through it and listen to everyone around me. I found me true purpose.

I am able to talk about Esports effortlessly. I know how to identify games for children and adults. Learning about Esports has brought me a lot of joy and closer to my children. I know there's still so much out there for me to learn, and I am going to keep reaching for new heights. When you stop learning, you stop living.

For me Esports was a relationship that festered a marriage of convenience. Whenever I talk about Esports, people can hear the passion in my voice and see it in my body motions. I was recently at a celebration where I was talking about what I do. The woman next to me said, "You are really passionate about this. I wish that I could be passionate about something like you." I explained to her how long it took me to get here, and that it was through several trials and tribulations that I was able to build a love for something that gives me so much joy.

Even to this day, my adult children are still amazed at what I know. They are still in denial. They were sitting in the living room talking about ranks in a particular video game, and without missing a beat, I said, "Are you playing Valorant?" My younger son said, "Yes," with a surprised look on his face. My older son said, "How do you know that?" I said, "Why don't you get it? I know Esports." I guess they can't see their mother in the world of Esports.

Esports is not something I do; it is who I have become.

Did You Follow Your Dreams?

Since I've been writing this book and talking about my children following their dreams, there have been numerous questions about me allowing my children to follow their paths. Parents wanted to know how I could allow my younger son to be a gamer, since I was such a strong, passionate parent who had raised honor students. My response to them was, "Did you follow your dreams? Did you become the person you wanted to be?"

I know I didn't follow my dreams. I wanted to work for the secret service. My family said that certain jobs were not for women, and that

I should be a nurse. I know, in a weird way, they were trying to look out for me, but they were stifling who I wanted to be. Well, as you know, I went into law enforcement anyway. I have always been a protector.

With that being said, I was not going to stop my children from following their dreams. I was not going to suppress them from becoming who they wanted to be. I may have slowed down the process a little bit, but once we got there, it was full steam ahead.

I unknowingly supported and encouraged a dream that was deep down in my child's heart. I remember the first time he met his favorite pro players at the tournament. It was just like when I met my favorite singer. The more I think about it, the more I see that there is no difference between an Esports player, an athlete or entertainer. Everyone is passionate about their craft. It was my inability to follow my dreams that pushed me in the direction of embracing what my children wanted to do.

Listen to Your Child

Esports has been an eye-opening experience, but if I had listened to my children in the beginning, it would not have been as difficult as I made it. It was like climbing the same mountain over and over again. As parents, we don't know everything, and sometimes it takes the smallest person or incident to help us see the full picture.

My journey was slow and captivating at the same time, but my ideology was governed by rules that did not exist in the world of

Esports. I needed to trust my children more. When I decided to go to OGF, it wasn't because I wanted to see what was happening; as you recall, I was prepared to read a book. I went to chaperone my children at the event, instead of supporting them. But the decision to go to OGF was a good one; it was one of the best times I have ever had in the world of Esports. My children told me it was exciting, but I couldn't see it. How could watching video games be exciting?

I had trusted my children with everything else, but why couldn't I trust them with this?

A child's minds are untainted, and they often tell and see the truth. We, as adults, often see the things that can go wrong, and not the fun we could have while playing a simple game. We have to understand that they may have a good idea and I know it can be scary to admit your child may be right.

Now, I want to be clear: It's your child and you know them better than anyone else. Not every idea is going to be a good.

Evaluate everything; just be a little more open to listen. Listening does not cost anything.

Conquer everything together.

Bonus 1 – Types of Scholarships

Do you have a child that is going to college or know someone that is going to college? Here are the different types of scholarships that are available:

- Athletic – includes Esports
- First Generation
- Academic
- Leaderships
- Volunteer
- Need Based
- Extracurricular Activities
- Military
- Stem
- Honor
- Major
- No Essay

Bonus 2 – Scholarships

Thousands of scholarships are left unawarded because no one applied for them. Here is a list of 25 scholarships you can apply for:

- Coca-Cola Scholars Foundation
- J.P. Morgan Chase
- Jovia Bank
- Hispanic Scholarship Fund
- McDonalds HACER Nation Scholarship
- The Burger King Scholars Programs
- The Barry Gold Scholarships
- The Gates Scholarship
- Goya Food Scholarship Program
- National Honor Society
- Prudential Emerging Visionaries
- The Cooke College Scholarship Program
- Island Federal Credit Union
- Ron Brown Scholar Program
- The Jackie Robinson Foundation Scholarship
- United States Hispanic Leadership Institute
- The Vegetarian Resource Group Scholarship
- Equitable Excellence Scholarship
- The Patrick McNeil Memorial Scholarship
- Foot Locker Scholar Athletes program
- Foundation for Fraternal Excellence Men's College Scholarship
- $1000 Jumpstart Scholarship
- 1 for 2 Education Foundation
- Clubs of America Scholarship Award for Career Success
- Corporate Culture Scholarship

Here are a few easy gaming terminologies:

An Esports Player is someone that plays video games on a highly competitive level.

A Gamer is a person that play video games via console, phone or other electronic devises. So, if you play Candy crush – you are a gamer.

Here are a few easy gaming terminologies:

- Esports: "Highly competitive video game Electronic sports"
- GG: "good game"
- IGN: In Game name
- Noob: Refers to a beginner or inexperienced player
- AFK: "Away from keyboard"
- FPS: "Frames per second"
- DPS: "Damage per second"
- MOBA: "Multiplayer online battle arena."
- APM: "Actions per minute"
- Ult: "Ultimate ability"
- Respawn: "The act of a player returning to the game after being eliminated or killed"
- Nerf: "When a character, weapon, or ability is intentionally weakened or made less effective by game developers"
- Crowd Control (CC): "Abilities or tactics that temporarily immobilize, silence, or disable opponents.
- Carry Role: "player deals significant damage and carries the team to victory"
- Gank: "When one or more players from a team ambush an opponent in a coordinated attack"
- Support Role: "player provides assistance, healing, or utility to their teammates"

Confessions of an Esports Mom

I wrote this letter to my gamer in June 2021

To our Gamer,

You have made us very proud with every step you make and every breath you take; your presence is always known.

We remember watching you strike out everyone when you were on the baseball mound. And now you are knocking them out in Esports. You may be quiet and shy, but your work speaks volumes of the young man you have become. The pandemic did not stop from being great. You push through and accomplished more than we could understand. Your passion for education and compassion for others is matchless.

We look forward to all the grand and glorious things you will do.

One day we will understand esports.

May our Lord and Savior bless everything you do.

Love you always, Mona and Dado

The idea to formulate my LLC came easy because
I knew parents needed help.
So, get ready to embark upon your new adventure
in the world of esports
and always remember I am here to help, visit me at:

www.bridging-the-Gap-in-Esports.com

Bridgingesports@gmail.com
@bridgingesports on IG and X

Made in the USA
Middletown, DE
22 February 2024

49540998R00075